INSPIRED BY MIRACLES

Inspired by Miracles

On Miracles, Relationships, and Inner Guidance

Dan Joseph

QUIET MIND PUBLISHING

Quiet Mind Publishing, LLC
PO Box 4024
Greenwich, CT 06831

(800) 758-5761 book orders (24 hrs/day)
email: info@quietmind.info

ISBN: 0-9716267-0-7
Library of Congress Control Number: 2001119823

If you would like information about featuring excerpts from this book,
please contact us at info@quietmind.info.

Permissions:

Excerpt from *You Can Be Happy No Matter What* ©1997 by Richard
Carlson. Reprinted with permission of New World Library, Novato,
CA.

Excerpt from *Meditations with Meister Eckhart* ©1982 by Matthew Fox.
Reprinted with permission of Inner Traditions / Bear & Co., Rochester,
VT.

A Course in Miracles ® © 1975, 1992, 1996 by the Foundation for A
Course in Miracles, Inc. A Course in Miracles ® is a registered trade-
mark of the Foundation for A Course in Miracles, Inc.

Please note that the ideas represented herein are the personal understanding of the author and are not necessarily endorsed by the copy-
right holder of *A Course in Miracles*.

FIRST PRINTING

CONTENTS

Author's Note

Inspired by Miracles is based on my work with *A Course in Miracles*, a program of "spiritual psychotherapy." The Course focuses on attaining peace of mind through practices such as forgiveness and prayer.

I'd like to be clear that I am no expert on *A Course in Miracles*. My perspectives on the Course are constantly evolving. Because of this, I encourage you to draw your own conclusions about the ideas that I share.

For those who are interested, I have included some companion material to *Inspired by Miracles* at www.DanJoseph.info. You are welcome to visit.

Preface

A teacher of mine once made an interesting point about language.

"Please imagine a tree," he said to our class.

We did as he asked.

"Now, because you live in the northeastern United States," he said, "chances are that you thought of a tree with green leaves. Am I right?"

We nodded – sure, we all thought of trees with green leaves.

"Did anyone think of an *evergreen* tree?" he asked. "A pine or fir tree?"

We shook our heads. None of us thought of an evergreen.

"Now, if you lived in Canada and I asked you to imagine a tree, things would have been different," he said. "In that case, many of you would have thought of an evergreen tree. The word is the same – 'tree.' But the pictures that came to mind would have been different."

He drew two trees on the chalkboard to illustrate.

"My point is," he concluded, pointing at the drawings, "if you were to have a conversation about 'trees' with a Canadian, you might be talking about two different things."

That lesson stayed with me because it shed some light on a common experience. I would often get involved in long discussions with people, only to find in the end that we were talking about different things. We were using the same words, but the "pictures" that we associated with the words were different.

I share this because any writing of a spiritual nature is prone to this. If two people can talk about trees and have different pictures in mind, how much wider is the potential for miscommunication when two people are talking about God, or prayer, or concepts like inner peace.

When I'm speaking with someone about the ideas from *A Course in Miracles*, I find that we occasionally need some back-and-forth clarification before we're "on the same page." Here is a simple example of what I mean:

Me: "I find that a key practice of the Course is prayer."

Friend: "Prayer? I don't like to pray. Prayer is just asking God for a bunch of things."

Me: "Actually, when I say 'prayer,' that's not what I mean."

Friend: "No? Then what do you mean?"

Me: "Well, prayer can be a practice of simply opening our hearts to the love of God."

Friend: "Oh, that sounds like what I call meditation. I didn't know that's what you meant by prayer."

And so on. The word "prayer" had different associations to us at the beginning. Through talking, we clarified our concepts a bit.

This works fine one-on-one, but in a book, the author has to guess where language problems may occur, and try to remedy them in advance. It's always a shot in the dark – guessing where any mismatches may be.

Because of this, I ask your forbearance. If there is an idea I express that doesn't fit with your understanding, we may be associating different meanings with certain words. Or we may have truly different perspectives. Either way, you're welcome to reinterpret anything I write in a way that feels correct to you.

At the outset, I would like to clarify my use of a couple of words. When I use the word "mind" in the writing that follows, I'm not referring to our human intellect. I use the words "mind" and "heart" fairly interchangeably.

When I say "mind," I mean the expansive place where thoughts, emotions, and visions are experienced.

In the following chapters, I also use the word God a great deal. The Course itself would use "the Holy Spirit" in many places where I use God, but for the sake of inclusiveness, I've decided to simply use God.

I'd like to add that although I sometimes refer to God as "He," I don't mean to promote an image of God as a man. The Course uses He, in keeping with traditional Judeo-Christian language. I use that convention because it is familiar to me. To be clear, I don't look at God as any more "masculine" than "feminine."

On a final note: I have, in general, leaned toward simplification in my presentation of the Course's ideas. For those who would like to explore *A Course in Miracles* a little deeper, I have included a Notes section at the end with additional commentary and section references to the Course itself.

One

Miracles

A Course in Miracles is a book about miracles. But what does the Course mean by a *miracle*?

A miracle, according to the Course, is an inner healing. A miracle is an experience of God's love. A miracle is what happens when we allow God to transform our thoughts and perspectives.

This is different than the traditional definition of a miracle. When people talk about "miracles," they usually mean events in the world — remarkable physical healings, for example. The Course, however, focuses on the inner experience that inspires those events.

Worldly healings are certainly wonderful. The Course wants every pain to be healed, and every conflict resolved.

But the Course teaches that true healing begins on the inside.

Miracles are inner experiences that bring peace to our minds and kindness to our hearts. They are rays of light that shine away our dark thoughts. They are gifts from God that help us to experience our lives in a completely new way.

The Course makes the important point that miracles – inner healings – are offered to us all the time. They are not rare and mysterious events. They come as soon as our minds are open to them.

Another important point is that miracles may not have any outwardly visible results. Miracles may simply help us to feel at peace. They may give us a sense that we're not alone.

Of course, worldly resolutions can occur as a result of a miracle. But even then, the resolution proceeds from the inside out. Let me offer a couple of examples to illustrate this process.

Let's imagine a woman who owns a business. This woman is stuck in a conflict with a business partner of hers. The conflict has been dragging on for weeks, and the woman feels exhausted.

In a last-ditch effort to resolve her problem, the woman shuts her office door, leans back in her chair, and says,

"God, please help." Then she sits for a few minutes with an open, receptive mind.

As the woman sits, a feeling of calm comes over her. Her perspective shifts, and she realizes that the business conflict isn't quite so threatening. Her shoulders relax. She takes a deep breath.

As the woman continues to sit, her mind clears. She begins to feel an increased sense of peace. Suddenly, an idea for a resolution to the conflict springs to mind.

In the end, the woman's business conflict is resolved. However, the resolution came because she let her mind be healed. The miracle was a touch of God that brought peace and clarity to the woman's mind. It was an inner experience that produced outer results.

Let me offer another illustration. Let's imagine a man who has a longstanding conflict with his wife. This man is always early for events, and his wife is always late. This is a source of irritation for both of them.

One day the man snaps at his wife about the issue. His wife snaps back at him, and they have an argument. Later on, the man feels terrible. He regrets the argument, and doesn't want to repeat the dynamic any longer.

The man sits down, closes his eyes, and says, "God, please give me a new way of looking at this. Please change my perspective." Then he rests for a minute in a state of open-mindedness.

As the man sits, his heart is unexpectedly flooded with a sense of appreciation for his wife. He is filled with a deep sense of love. Issues of being on time seem meaningless by comparison.

After a minute, the man opens his eyes. He tells his wife that he loves her, and that the issue no longer matters. She nevertheless expresses to him that she'll try to be on time. They both feel supported. Their relationship is restored to peace.

In that situation, the conflict was resolved through a miracle – a healing of the mind and heart. The outer relationship was changed, but the change began on the inside.

The miracle was the touch of God that brought a flood of love into the man's heart. Although the miracle did produce external results, it was an inner experience. It came when the man opened his heart to it.

The Course wants us to realize that miracles are not things that we generate by ourselves. In the example above, the business owner didn't try to "force" herself into a state of clarity. Instead, she simply turned to God with an open mind. The husband didn't try to "ramp up" a sense of appreciation for his wife. He simply opened his heart to the inflow of God's love.

The Course teaches that miracles – God's loving thoughts – will come to us when our minds and hearts are open. Our job is simply to clear the way for them.

Our Part in the Process

According to the Course, God loves us and wants us to be at peace. God wants us to feel comforted and cared for. He gives us miracles to heal our minds of any thought that causes us distress.

The problem, says the Course, is that we often close our minds to miracles. Whenever we fill our minds with our own dark thoughts, we're temporarily passing up an opportunity to receive a miracle.

We are given this freedom. We have the choice to accept whatever thoughts we wish. But it is important to realize that the choice is ours. God does not withhold miracles from us. He offers them at every moment. It's up to us to decide when to accept them.

What does it look like to be closed to miracles? As an example, let's imagine that I dislike my job. I consider it to be boring and meaningless.

However, whenever anyone suggests that I look for a new job, I say, "Oh, no – you don't understand. Someone in my situation can't find anything new."

That attitude is a block to the experience of a miracle. Although God wishes to comfort and guide me, He will not force His miracles into my closed mind. He respects my choices and will wait for an opening.

Let's imagine that I hold onto my old attitudes for years. Then, one day, I have a conversation with a co-worker.

"Same stuff, different day," I say.

"You don't like your job?" asks my co-worker.

"No," I say, "but what can you do. I can't find anything new."

"I used to feel that way," says my co-worker, "but one day I hit a point where I couldn't take it anymore. I decided that there *had* to be something better in life. Soon after that, I found a new job."

"You found something new?"

"Something great. I love my work now."

That conversation begins to open my mind. I respect my co-worker's experience, especially because she was once in a similar situation.

"Who knows," I say, shrugging. "Perhaps there *is* a chance that I could find something new." As I say that, I feel a lightening in my heart. That opening of the heart is the invitation to a miracle.

Later that day, the idea for a new career path springs to mind – seemingly out of the blue. A feeling of peace comes over me. I catch a glimpse of how things could work out. "Goodness," I say. "Perhaps I've been wrong all these years about my opportunities."

That shift of perspective is the result of a miracle. It came quickly when I opened my mind. While my mind remained locked onto my old thoughts and attitudes, there wasn't an opening. But as my mind opened, the miracle found a way in.

This is why so much of the Course focuses on helping us to release our personal perspectives. It can be a humbling process. When we're feeling upset, the last thing we want to do is consider that there may be another way to think about our problem.

Nevertheless, there comes a time when, perhaps through sheer exhaustion, we begin to open our minds to a new perspective. That moment is the invitation to God to step in.

Giving and Receiving

A Course in Miracles offers many insights on receiving miracles. One of my favorites is this: whatever we *give* to others, we strengthen for ourselves.

I saw this dynamic illustrated very clearly when I worked as a tutor for high school students. As tutors, one of our practices was to turn our students into teachers.

We would begin by teaching the material to our students. Then we would ask the students to teach the material right back to *us*. As the students taught us the material, they strengthened it for themselves.

The Course says that this giving-is-strengthening idea can be used in regard to miracles. If we offer miracles to others, we will open our own minds to miracles in the process. If we allow ourselves to become conduits for God's love, we will experience this same love ourselves.

I had an interesting experience with this idea several years ago. I realized, one day, that I had made a bad business decision – a mistake that would cost me some money. I became very upset with myself. Although I tried to release my anger, I couldn't seem to let it go.

Hours later, while driving around, I realized I was still quite mad. I also recognized that it wasn't a great idea to drive around feeling upset. (I remembered my driver's education teacher saying, "If you break up with your girl-friend and tears are coming down your cheeks – pull over and have a good cry. Don't drive.")

I decided to pull over and take a few minutes of prayer time. I said, "God, I am really upset at myself. I made a mistake. Please help me find some peace." Unfortunately, nothing seemed to happen. Although I said the words, I was still angry.

A funny thing happened a few minutes later, though. I walked into a store and felt inspired to hold the door for a person behind me. Suddenly, about half my anger vanished. It was like magic.

I stood there, holding the door for anyone who came by. The rest of my anger quickly drained away. After a minute, I felt great. I decided that I had found the quickest, easiest form of psychotherapy ever invented.

In that situation, I needed an extra boost. I was upset, and couldn't let go of my anger. I couldn't open my mind to a miracle – an inner healing. But the simple act of holding a door helped me to open my mind. I extended a small act of help, and in the process, I opened to God's great help.

Speaking broadly, it could be said that every kind thought is a miracle. With every kind thought we give, we receive one as well. Of course, as I mentioned earlier, the Course doesn't require us to generate kind thoughts all by ourselves. It simply asks us to let God's kindness flow through us.

We can choose to offer miracles – reflections of God's love – to whoever needs help. Let me present an illustration of this process.

Let's imagine a woman who is an attorney. This woman receives a phone call from her father one day. Her father is upset because a neighbor is beginning construction on a house, and he fears that there will be a great deal of noise.

"Can I sue my neighbor to stop this?" he asks his daughter.

The woman loves her father, and wants to help him. However, she knows that a lawsuit won't resolve the problem. She begins to explain the details of the law. But then she stops and says silently, "God, please enter here and help my father."

In that moment her mind rests and becomes open. She is suddenly flooded with a sense of warmth.

"Dad," she says, "I've really missed seeing you. Perhaps if there is noise next door, you'll think about spending time with us. We really love to see you, and it would be great to see you more."

The warmth behind that statement is the reflection of a miracle – a reflection of God's love. It came because the woman wished to help her father, and chose to open to God's help. She served as a conduit for God's loving thoughts.

As I mentioned earlier, miracles may not have outwardly visible results. The father may hang up the phone and still be upset at his neighbor. There may not be any obvious changes from the conversation.

Nevertheless, the woman has done her job. She has stopped and asked God for a miracle. She has opened her mind to receive it, and has offered what she received. The warmth of God's love will stay with her. The father will be touched by the miracle as well, to whatever degree that his own mind is open.

There are two important steps in this process. First, the woman realized that her father needed a miracle – an experience of God's love. Second, she opened her own mind to receive and extend that love. She didn't try to talk her father out of his anger, or otherwise tackle things in her own way. She placed herself – at least for a moment – in service to God, and thus became a miracle worker.

We ourselves need miracles all the time. As we see that those around us need miracles, too – and we allow ourselves to become conduits for those miracles – we will fulfill our own need. Offering miracles to others is one of the greatest gifts we can give to ourselves.

I feel that as we practice receiving and offering miracles, it's important to keep our focus on the internal experience. I try to avoid analyzing whether the miracle "worked" to solve an outer problem. Miracles may resolve deeper problems than the ones we're focused on. Even if there doesn't seem to be any external change in a situation, there may be deep internal changes going on.

If we make an effort to turn over the situations in our lives to God, and open to receive (and extend) His loving thoughts, we are doing an excellent job.

Application

I feel that discussing the ideas in the Course – including the Course's ideas on miracles – is helpful. It is like studying a map before taking a trip.

However, I find that the Course's ideas have little impact if they remain as theory. We need to *apply* the ideas to our lives if we wish to feel a change. I struggled with this for years, thinking that intellectual understanding was all the Course asked. I was definitely wrong.

When I began working with the Course, I was in college. At that time, I treated the Course like an academic subject. It was something to be read, analyzed, and discussed. It was a fascinating book of ideas.

The problem with my "academic" approach was that I never ended up *using* the Course's ideas. They remained as mere intellectual concepts.

My approach provoked a few chuckles. Every few days, I'd become inspired by an idea in the Course. I'd call up a friend of mine and ask him to meet me for coffee. When we got together, I would excitedly launch into a presentation of the brilliant idea I had just read.

My friend would listen attentively. He'd nod his head. Then he'd begin to smile. "That's really great," he'd say when I was finished. "But Dan, didn't you tell me the same thing *last* week?"

My friend was right. There were different flavors from week to week, but the truth was that I kept stumbling back and forth between bright ideas and darkness. I never stopped to ask myself, "How can I *use* these ideas? How can I make them a real part of my life?"

Working with the Course on a purely intellectual level was like sitting around in a cave, lighting matches. When a match was lit, everything seemed so clear. I wanted to rush around and share the light with everyone. But then the match would go out, and I'd find myself back in darkness.

I never thought to apply the flame – to build a fire to provide lasting warmth. Yet that is exactly what the Course is asking us to do.

Today, I look at the Course as a set of tools. The Course has some brilliant insights and ideas. But they are building blocks for the inner work. It is this inner work that will accomplish the real changes.

It's one thing, for example, to read about entrusting our lives to God. It's another thing to sit down and take an inventory of the areas where we're *not* trusting God, and begin to hand those areas over. That proactive work is what the Course is asking us to do.

Of course, I do think that understanding the Course's ideas is helpful. This process requires some reading and study. But we can learn an idea in one moment, and immediately begin to apply it in the next. That, in my opinion, is the real practice of the Course.

As an assistance to this, I like to develop exercises based on the Course's ideas. These exercises help me – and hopefully others – bring the Course's ideas to a practical level.

In this book, I'd like to present a dozen simple exercises that are aimed at helping us open to the inner experience of a miracle. This is where my true enjoyment comes from, for I see the value of this type of work.

An Exercise

In the process of opening to miracles, I often find that it's helpful for me to write down my thoughts. Writing down my thoughts can help me to clarify any "blocks" to a miracle.

For example: I may be feeling irritable one day. Someone asks me, "Is something wrong?" and I tell her, "No – nothing's wrong." I'm simply feeling irritable. I can't come up with a specific issue that's bothering me.

However, if I were to sit down and write out my thoughts, I might find a number of issues that are contributing to my irritability. Perhaps they are so minor that I've "dismissed" them. Yet they continue to trouble me.

In my minute of writing, I might realize that I'm mad that my favorite baseball team lost, and I'm frustrated that

I can't find my good socks. That's it.

I may have dismissed both of those situations as "unimportant" when they happened. However, I kept hold of the underlying irritation. Bringing my thoughts back into focus can help me to *truly* release the issues, along with the attendant irritation.

It is, of course, possible to be so aware of our thoughts that we don't have to use a technique like writing. However, almost everyone I know benefits from the greater sense of focus that writing imparts.

Having said that, I'd like to present a simple exercise that involves some writing. This exercise supports us in opening our minds to the healing experience of a miracle.

You are welcome, of course, to work with this exercise in whatever way feels meaningful. You don't have to actually write down your thoughts if you don't wish. However, I personally find that writing helps me to focus and clarify my mind.

Often when I do this exercise – and actually write out my thoughts – I'm surprised at the issues that surface. I say, "Wow, I didn't know that I was thinking *that*." Becoming clear about our thoughts can help us identify any blocks to the experience of a miracle. This allows us to clear an opening for God's inspired thoughts.

For those who would like to simply read through this exercise (and the ones that follow), I have included a sample response after each step. I will discuss this italicized example at the end.

Step 1. Let's begin by choosing a situation in our lives that is causing some distress. It could be a situation that's causing us anxiety, anger, or sadness.

(ex. My stock market portfolio got crushed last week.)

Step 2. Why is this situation troubling? Even if it seems "obvious," it can be helpful to identify our actual thoughts about the situation. We may not realize the full extent of what we're thinking until we articulate our specific thoughts.

This step calls for a great deal of honesty. Let's write out our thoughts about why this situation is troubling using the format, "This situation *shows that...*"

(ex. This situation shows that it's difficult to make money, and when you do, it can all be taken away. It shows that I'm bad at investing. It shows that I always make mistakes with money.)

Step 3. Step two was designed to clarify some of the personal thoughts (or interpretations) that we have about our situation. If we're doing this exercise correctly, we may be surprised at what surfaced. Once we have clarified our own personal thoughts, we can begin our work.

Having clarified some of our thoughts and interpretations, let's now ask ourselves: "Can I trade these thoughts for something more peaceful? Am I willing to accept a new set of thoughts from God?"

As we consider those questions, we may find ourselves saying, "Who cares about my thoughts. This problem has nothing to do with my thoughts." The Course, however, feels otherwise.

We can't accept miracles – inner healings – if our minds are tightly holding onto our own dark thoughts. We need to give God room to enter. We need to at least begin to clear a space in our minds for a miracle.

If we find ourselves willing to open our minds – even just a little – let's say a brief introductory prayer:

God, I am upset about this situation.
But I accept that there may be another way to think
    about it.
I am willing to exchange my thoughts for yours.
Please offer me a miracle to heal my mind.

Then let's take a full minute to give over our old thoughts to God. This is the real work. Our goal in this minute is to release our old attitudes, and become open to the inflow of God's loving, inspired thoughts – God's miracles.

This does take some effort. It requires some focus. But our goal is simply to clear our minds of our old, personal thoughts, and open our hearts to God's comforting replacements. It can be a very restful practice.

If it helps, we can use imagery in this process. For example, we can envision ourselves giving over our thoughts to God as if they were objects in our hands. Or we can see ourselves wading into a river, and allowing God to wash away our personal interpretations of the situation.

Imagery isn't essential, but it can help us make this process more concrete. Either way, our focus is on handing over our personal thoughts about the situation, and opening to God's new thoughts.

As we sit for a minute, practicing this exchange, we may begin to feel a sense of peace come over us. If so, that is wonderful. Peace is our goal. A sense of peace is the indication that our minds are opening to a miracle. That peace – if we let it – will stay with us. It can clear the way for inspired new thoughts as we go forward.

If we try to do this exercise and *don't* feel any increase in peace, it doesn't mean that we've failed. The simple act of identifying our thoughts about the situation is a powerful step. Sitting quietly for a minute, seeking God's comfort, is of great value – regardless of whether or not we feel that we've "arrived."

The key in this type of exercise is to practice. The Course suggests that we build a habit of turning to God whenever we are upset. Our efforts to practice are well spent, regardless of our apparent level of "success." If we like, we can repeat this exercise (or one like it) a few times a day, and see if it becomes easier as we go along.

To shed more light on this simple practice, let me discuss the italicized example that I gave in the exercise.

In the example, the person experienced an upsetting stock market loss. But there were really two things going on. There was a worldly event: in this case, a stock market downturn. Then, immediately after that, there was an inner response of pessimistic thoughts.

I don't mean to suggest that this is unusual. Many of us would have a similar response. However, these pessimistic thoughts are the real problem – they are the block to the miracle. God's love can't enter our awareness if we're clinging tightly to our own negative thoughts.

The person in the example is asked to separate out his thoughts *about* the stock market event from the event itself, and then offer those thoughts to God in exchange for a miracle. He is asked to clear out a space in his mind for God's peace to enter.

Although this exercise is simple, it's not always easy. It can be particularly difficult to do when we're in a state of emotional distress. The person with the stock market loss may be angry. He may say, "I don't know what my 'thoughts' are. I just feel terrible. I'd be lying to myself if I said I wasn't upset."

I want to be clear that the Course is never asking us to deny our emotions. It isn't asking us to put on a happy face when we do this practice, or pretend we feel OK when we really don't. The Course asks us, in fact, to be extremely honest about our feelings. They can serve as excellent indicators of what we're thinking.

Before going any further, I'd like to discuss the relationship between thoughts and emotions that the Course outlines. It may provide some helpful insights on the process of opening to miracles.

Thoughts and Emotions

Dark emotions can be challenging to deal with – especially strong emotions like fear, anger, and despair. When we're upset, these types of emotions can overwhelm us, creating a cloud between us and the miracle.

The Course doesn't want us to deny our emotions, no matter how dark or scary they may be. But it does want us to look at the relationship between what we're *feeling* and what we're *thinking*. According to the Course, our emotions simply follow from our thoughts.

Emotions, according to the Course, do not wash randomly over us. Rather, they stem from our thoughts. This can be difficult to see – particularly when we're feeling upset. However, it can be a helpful step toward opening to a miracle.

The psychologist Richard Carlson has written extensively about the relationship between thoughts and emotions. In his book *You Can Be Happy No Matter What*, he writes:

> Every negative (and positive) feeling is a direct result of thought. It's impossible to have jealous feelings without first having jealous thoughts, to have sad feelings without first having sad thoughts, to feel angry without having angry thoughts. And it's impossible to be depressed without having depressing thoughts. This seems obvious, but if it were better understood, we would all be happier and live in a happier world!

He then describes a typical interchange with a client, in which the client expresses that he's been feeling depressed but can't see that he's been *thinking* depressing *thoughts*.

Many of us have trouble seeing this. Yet if we can identify the thoughts (or interpretations) that are producing our emotions, we may be more able to open our minds to the healing experience of a miracle.

As an illustration of this, let's imagine that I am upset because someone was rude to me. I stomp around all day, muttering under my breath.

"What's wrong?" someone asks me.

"I'll tell you," I say. "So-and-so was rude to me. She said this and that. Can you believe it? That's why I'm upset."

But I am wrong. I'm not upset *right now* because someone said something earlier that day. I am upset because of the thoughts I am carrying around. Until I realize that, I won't even think to open my mind to a miracle.

Perhaps a few hours later I'm feeling a little clearer. I'm still upset, but I'm more aware of the dynamic.

"What's wrong?" someone asks.

"Well," I say, "I'll tell you. So-and-so was rude to me, and that bothered me. But what's bothering me now is that I've decided that people in general are insensitive. I think that I'm surrounded by rude people. Those thoughts are what's bothering me."

Once the problem is set up in that way, the solution becomes clear. I can turn to God and say, "God, please heal my mind with a miracle." The problem isn't what someone said to me earlier that day. The problem is that my mind is filled with dark thoughts right now.

Did the other person "spark" my dark thoughts with her behavior? Perhaps. But I have to take responsibility for my current state of mind, and ask God for healing. If I remain fixated on the event itself – rather than my thoughts *about* the event – I will never stop to let my mind be healed. I will simply continue to believe that the problem is the other person.

Our bad feelings are usually sparked by troubling events – losses, conflicts, and so forth. But the Course is asking us to realize that there is a razor-thin moment between the event and our feelings in which we make an *interpretation*. That interpretation is the real cause of our feelings. That interpretation can be transformed by a miracle.

Here is a simple diagram to illustrate the flow of things:

Event

↓

Our thoughts *about* the event or
interpretations *of* the event

↓

Emotions

The miracle works primarily on that middle tier. It unhooks us from our negative thoughts, and thus lets our hearts return to peace.

I don't want to make it sound as though this process is easy. When we're upset, it can be extremely challenging to identify our thoughts, and turn to God for healing. There is a significant temptation to say, "My thoughts have no bearing on this. The problem is entirely so-and-so past event, or so-and-so other person."

The problem is that we stay stuck if we insist that we're upset because of something completely external to ourselves. Another person or a worldly event may have sparked our negative reaction. Sometimes it's quite difficult to avoid this. But when we're ready, we can exchange our thoughts for an inner healing – a miracle.

I'd like to be clear that as we go through our lives we will likely make some dark interpretations and have some negative thoughts. This, in my opinion, isn't the real problem. The real problem is that we tend to *hold onto* those thoughts and interpretations – often for quite a long time.

If the stock market crashed, for example, and a person said, "Oh no, this is a horrible thing! I'm going to lose my chance to buy that house I wanted!" – and yet, a few minutes later said, "Well, you know, perhaps I'm wrong. Maybe there's another interpretation here," all would be fine. There was a temporary block to God's comfort and healing, but then the person opened that block to question.

The real problem occurs when we form an interpretation and lock it in. Perhaps the stock market crashes, and we say, "Oh no. This is devastating. I've lost everything. There's no hope for me anymore."

Sorrowful emotions will begin to layer over that interpretation, and our minds will gather evidence to "prove" that the interpretation is correct. Years may pass, and unless we allow that interpretation to be transformed by a miracle, it will remain.

Our thoughts, or interpretations, can be changed at any moment. But we need to open the door to this process. Miracles – God's loving thoughts – are waiting for an entrance. We simply need to let them in by creating a space of open-mindedness.

Perspectives

The Course says that our thoughts and interpretations are so powerful that they not only influence our emotions – they actually color everything we see.

Once we have chosen an interpretation of an event, that interpretation tends to create a "perspective." From then on, we see the event only through the lens of our personal perspectives on it. Our perspectives are so powerful that we never really see past them.

The Course acknowledges this, and asks us to trade our personal perspectives for God's wider vision. We can say, "God, how would *you* have me look at this?" Opening to a miracle can be as simple as that.

Let me offer a couple of personal examples on the power of perspectives.

Years ago, I was involved in an arrangement with a business associate of mine. We agreed to share the work on a project, and split the fee from our client.

When the project was complete, however, I didn't receive my half of the payment. I called up my associate and we had a conversation that went like this.

"Hi," I said. "I'm just calling to check on the payment."

"Yes," said my associate. "I'm sorry to tell you this, but I'm keeping your half."

"You're what?"

"I'm keeping your half of the money," he said.

Thus began a very acrimonious couple of months. I argued repeatedly with my associate, threatened to take him to court, and generally worked myself into a state of misery.

As time went by, I increasingly perceived this man as my enemy. I saw him as the source of all the major problems in my life. Every time I reinvested in that perspective, I found more "evidence" to support it.

Then, one day, I had a conversation with my associate. In a moment of great honesty, he confided that his business was failing, that he was being audited by the IRS, and that he was in danger of losing his home.

My perspective immediately shifted. Suddenly I saw the man not as a powerful enemy, but as someone who was frightened and looking for help. As my view of the situation shifted, my anger changed to compassion.

The Course talks a great deal about this type of shift. We see people as threats, but miracles help us to see their calls for help. This new perspective fosters an increased sense of peace and clarity.

In my situation, the new perspective inspired a mutually acceptable solution to our business conflict. In the end, things worked out fine between us.

The key, however, was the shift in perspective. If I had held onto my old view – and the anger that came with it – I might still be fighting with my associate today.

As a similar example, I recently received a contribution from a creative partner of mine. I felt that there were some problems in the work that needed to be addressed, and I was a bit annoyed.

I contacted my partner to discuss the situation, and learned that he had spent the last few weeks tending to his wife, who was ill. My annoyance was immediately replaced with a desire to support him. The sudden shift in perspective made the creative problems seem meaningless.

Situations like those have happened many times. It's actually remarkable that I still lock onto my personal perspectives – I have seen that my views are always incomplete, to some degree. The Course is asking us to realize this, and accept God's wider vision.

In the examples above, I was able to accept a shift in perspective because I learned something about the situations of the other people involved. However, a miracle can make this shift for us internally, if we will let it. We don't have to wait for new outside information. All that we need do is loosen our grasp on our current perspectives, and ask God to inspire a new view. He will respond to this invitation.

A Variation

I'd like to offer a variation on the earlier exercise I presented. The earlier exercise focused on the thoughts we held about a situation. This one focuses on our *view* of a situation. The goal in this exercise is to let our perspectives, or views, be transformed by God.

As I mentioned earlier, you're free to work with these exercises in whatever way is personally meaningful.

Step 1. One area of my life that really bothers me is:

(ex. I really don't like spending time with my in-laws. I don't like having them visit.)

Step 2. If I had to describe how I *see* this situation (including the people involved in it), I would say:

(ex. I see it as a very irritating situation. I see my in-laws as rude and uncaring. I see them as uninterested in me.)

Step 3. Because our perspectives are so powerful, they color everything we see. In order to accept God's peace-producing perspective on this situation, we need to be willing to release our own not-so-peaceful perspectives.

Let's ask ourselves: Am I willing to accept that there might be a different way to look at this situation – even though there may be a good deal of "evidence" for my current perspective?

If we are willing to consider a new, more peaceful perspective, let's say:

God, I am troubled by this area of my life.
However, I am willing to see it in a new way.
Please exchange my view of this situation for your view.
Heal my vision with a miracle.

Then let's spend a full minute in silence, saying this to God in our hearts. We'll know we're on the right track if we begin to feel an increased sense of peace. Our goal in this step is to open ourselves to God's broader view of the situation. As we adopt God's view, we are letting our minds be healed.

As I mentioned in the earlier exercise, we may want to use imagery in this process. Imagery isn't essential, but it can help us stay focused.

We can imagine ourselves, for example, removing an old set of eyeglasses and accepting a new, clearer set of glasses from God. Our current view of this situation causes us distress. God's view of the same situation will inspire compassion and peace. As we become willing to trade our personal views for God's compassionate vision, we will see things much more clearly.

As we sit for a minute, handing over our old views to God, we may experience a sudden shift into a new perspective. Or we may only begin to feel a slight amount of lightening. Either of these is fine.

Our goal in these exercises is simply to move in a new direction. If we feel a tiny bit of lightening, and we hold that course, we may find that a few days from now there is quite a bit more light.

As the Course points out, our willingness to accept God's help is the key. If we do nothing but sit and increase our willingness to receive God's miracle-inspired vision, we are doing excellent work.

As I mentioned earlier, it can be tough to identify what our personal perspectives are. In the example that I gave above, it may have required a lot of honesty for the person to admit that she saw her in-laws as rude and uncaring. The temptation is to say, "I'm not *seeing* them as rude and uncaring – they just *are* rude and uncaring."

The people in our lives may indeed be exhibiting rude and uncaring behavior. However, we're still called upon to take responsibility for our perception of the situation, and offer that perception to God. The miracle will heal our minds and reorient our views, regardless of what's happening on the outside.

Let me address a common form of resistance to this practice. Some people, when they try to do this exercise, say, "Frankly, I don't care about changing my *perspective*. I just want the *situation* to be changed."

This is a very honest response. However, the Course makes a good point in this regard. If we don't let our minds be healed by a miracle, and we instead simply manipulate the outer situation, we'll probably find ourselves confronted with a similar situation later on.

As an illustration of this, let's imagine that the person with the difficult in-laws sits down with her husband. She says, "Sweetheart, I don't want to invite your parents over to the house. They're always rude to me." He agrees, and the situation seems resolved. However, this person still dreads an unexpected visit from her in-laws. She also feels some guilt about her decision.

Additionally, a few months later, new neighbors move in next door who have a temperament that is remarkably similar to the in-laws. The woman feels as though her problem is "following her." This type of situation is calling for a miracle – an inner healing – rather than a mere external restructuring.

I feel that it's important for us to be gentle with ourselves in this process. As we're working toward a change of mind, we don't have to fight our way through uncomfortable situations. The person in the example may wish to take a temporary break from her in-laws. This isn't a problem. It may, in fact, be the best thing to do.

The Course is guiding us toward a state of peace – a state of true peace that comes from God, born of a new perspective. While we're working toward this fundamental change, we're encouraged to be kind to ourselves. However, we do, ultimately, need to let our minds be healed.

Valuation

If I'm having difficulty opening my mind to a new perspective, I often find it helpful to look at how much value I'm placing on my *old* ways of seeing. Sometimes we invest very heavily in our old perspectives, without even knowing it.

For example, let's say that I'm having trouble with my boss at work. I see my boss as demanding and arrogant. I take responsibility for those perceptions, and turn to God with them. I say, "God, please give me another way of seeing my boss. I want a new perspective."

Unfortunately, nothing seems to happen. My boss continues to be demanding, and I still feel upset.

Then, one day, I sit down with a co-worker. My co-worker says, "Hey – don't we have a great boss?"

"A *great boss*?" I say. "Are you kidding?"

"Sure," my co-worker says. "I mean, she has that rough personality at first. But I just kept reaching past that. I'd say that we're real friends now."

I'm taken aback. "Friends?" I say. "My goodness. I could never be *friends* with our boss. I mean, if we were friends then I'd have to take on extra work."

That, perhaps, is my problem. Part of my mind has been valuing my old perceptions of my boss in order to protect myself from "having to take on extra work." If I can accept that the miracle won't require me to be a door-mat for my boss, I may be more inclined to accept an inner healing.

Many of us fall into this trap. On one level, we want our minds to be healed. We want to be at peace. But on another level, we're frightened of what will happen if we release our own, personal perspectives. I think that it's important to be very honest with ourselves about our resistance. Once we lift up these blocks to our awareness, we can ask God for help in releasing them.

As another illustration, let's imagine a woman who is generally gentle and calm. This woman, however, has a recurring issue in her life. She sees reckless, dangerous drivers on the road everywhere. She sometimes gets into heated arguments with them.

The woman decides that she wants this area of her life to be healed. She turns to God with the problem. She says, "God, I think that most drivers are crazy. But I'm willing to receive a new perspective on this. Please heal my mind." Unfortunately, nothing seems to happen. The woman doesn't feel any more peaceful, and the drivers keep bothering her.

One day she's cut-off by a man who abruptly crosses several lanes of traffic. At the next light, she pulls next to the man and opens her window. "How dare you drive like that!" she says. She scolds him until he drives away. As she's heading home, the woman realizes that she feels energized and alive.

Later that day, the woman takes a moment to reflect on her situation. "Perhaps I'm *looking* for an excuse to vent some of my emotions," she says to herself. "Perhaps that's why I'm always focusing on bad drivers. However, this is a dangerous dynamic. I'd rather find safer ways to express myself."

That woman, using a great deal of honesty, identified a block to the miracle. As long as she continued to derive value from her old perceptions, she had trouble exchanging them for an inner healing. But when she realized that she didn't need an "excuse" to express her emotions, she became more willing to let her perceptions be changed.

In both of these examples – me with my boss, the woman with the drivers – we needed to identify the sense of value that was linked to our old thoughts and perceptions. In my case, the "value" of the old perspective was protection against imagined increased work. In the woman's case, the "value" was having an environment in which to express her emotions.

If we find ourselves resistant to exchanging our personal perspectives for God's healing vision, we may want to look for any value we're associating with our old ways of seeing. Once that "value" is raised to the light, we may realize that it doesn't outweigh the peace of a miracle.

Ordinary Things

When I discuss the process of receiving a miracle – an inner healing – I don't mean to limit our focus to troubling areas. Miracles can help light up the ordinary aspects of our lives as well.

To illustrate this, I'd like to offer a final variation of the previous exercises. Although similar in structure to the earlier ones, this exercise deals with an "ordinary" area.

Step 1. Here is an area of my life that feels rather "ordinary" or "neutral":

(ex. My carpentry business feels ordinary. It doesn't thrill me, but it's fine.)

Step 2. Here is how I *view* that area of my life:

(ex. I view it as just a business. I view it as a good way to make money. I sometimes view it as a pain, but it's OK.)

Step 3. Am I willing to let God transform this area of my life? Am I willing to be shown it brand-new, in a way that will bring me joy? If so, let me say:

God, this area of my life seems quite ordinary.
However, it only seems that way because of my thoughts
*   about it.*
Please take this area and transform my view of it.
I want to see it as you would have me see it.

Then let's give over our perceptions of this area – however neutral or ordinary they may be. Let's take a full minute to let God show us some bright spark in it that we may have never noticed before.

This type of exercise can have unexpected results. Our view of an "ordinary" thing can be transformed into a vision of something quite beautiful and lovely. The value of an exercise like this is that it allows us to work with an area of our lives that isn't emotionally charged.

The idea for this exercise came to me while standing in a parking lot. There was a brief moment in which my mind opened to receive God's perspective – at least, to some degree. Suddenly, everything looked very lovely. The cars, the flowers around the store, the people walking by, the breeze – it was touching. It seemed so nice. There seemed to be a kindness in all things.

That was a small taste of what God's vision reveals to us. The miracle clears our minds and shows us the presence of gentleness everywhere. It promotes a vision that mystics have written about – a vision that sees God's glory in little things.

This vision was expressed very beautifully by the fourteenth century German mystic Meister Eckhart, who wrote:

Every single creature is full of God and is a book
    about God.
Every creature is a word of God.
If I spent enough time with the tiniest creature –
even a caterpillar – I would never have to prepare
    a sermon, so full of God is every creature.

That is the type of perspective that the miracle calls forth. Of course, this vision isn't reserved for fourteenth century priests; it is a vision that God is constantly offering to all of us. God's miracles can lighten our sight and guide our perception so that we see wonder and beauty at every turn.

To Meister Eckhart, let me add a similar fragment from the poet Walt Whitman:

To me every hour of the light and dark is a miracle,
Every cubic inch of space is a miracle,
Every square yard of the surface of the earth is spread
    with the same,
Every foot of the interior swarms with the same.
To me the sea is a continual miracle.

When I was young, a teacher of mine said, "Only the poets and the mystics can see clearly." Perhaps he was right, but we can each share that vision as we allow God's miracles to cleanse our minds and guide our sight. That vision is not reserved for a select few. God offers it to everyone.

To return to the exercise above: the person in the example experienced his carpentry business as rather ordinary. Looking a little deeper, he admitted that he was choosing to *view* it in an ordinary way, as most of us do with our business affairs. If, however, he became willing to let his perceptions of the business be transformed by a miracle, he might have found himself beholding a lovely, remarkable thing.

I imagine that each of us allows this to happen in little ways, every day. A grandmother who sees a shining light in her granddaughter is using this vision. A teacher who finds delight in the innocence of her students is opening her mind to a wider perspective. For many of us, these moments of vision are the things of real value in the world.

Little Steps

A Course in Miracles encourages us to take gradual, steady steps toward a new perspective. We can let our minds be healed in little ways every day.

We can begin the perspective-changing process by letting God elevate our views of ordinary things. As we offer God our views of "little" things to be transformed, we may find it easier to turn over the "larger" things in our lives as well.

As an illustration of this practice, let's imagine a woman who owns a store. This woman dreads interacting with her landlord, as he often criticizes the way she runs her store. The woman tries to avoid the man, but she occasionally has to speak with him about business matters.

One day, the woman has an appointment to meet her landlord. As a preparation for the meeting, she decides to spend the day receiving miracles. "God," she says, "show me the beauty of everyone who walks into my store today. Help me to see everything through your eyes."

The woman repeats her prayer throughout the day. As each customer walks in, she says, "How should I see this person? How would you have me look at this one?"

The woman practices diligently, and her mind begins to open to an innocent beauty in everyone she meets. Miracles transform her view. The people who walk in her door are no longer customers; they are friends. Her store is no longer a place of business; it is a place of kindness. She is filled with a quiet sense of joy.

Late in the day, the woman's landlord walks in. She initially returns to her old perception of him. But then the momentum of her practice kicks in, and she allows the new vision to take hold.

As the landlord rattles on about the rent, the woman begins to perceive him differently. He seems like a frightened child, blustery in his fear. Yet he has the same spark of innocence that the others do. For the first time, she sees it.

Perhaps the landlord will stop blustering and say, "You know, things feel a little different around here today." Or perhaps he will keep acting as he always has.

Either way, the woman's mind has been healed. She has received miracles — first in regard to her customers, and then in regard to one who troubled her. Her mind has been restored to peace by taking "little steps."

Two Types of Vision

The Course suggests that there are two basic ways of looking at the world. If we see the world through miracles — through the peaceful mind and forgiving heart that miracles give us — the world can seem to sparkle. If we see the world through a cloud of conflict and dark thoughts, the world will seem hopeless and gray.

I find myself vacillating between these two ways of seeing, often quite sharply. There will be a day when I spend a few hours with a friend. I feel peaceful and spiritually connected. The world looks very hopeful. There seems to be a potential for goodness everywhere.

Then, things will shift. Perhaps I get into an argument with someone. My mind becomes clouded. The world, which just a few minutes ago looked hopeful, suddenly seems dangerous and dark. I see potential for threat everywhere.

It can be an important part of the process for us to experience the difference between these two ways of seeing. Our perceptions of the world are always colored, to some degree, by the thoughts we hold in mind. We either see the world through our dark thoughts, or through the light of miracles.

At the beginning of this process, we may feel as though we're stuck in a fixed, gray world. Life seems drab and beyond any hope of change. But as we begin to experience the sharp contrast between our normal thoughts and miracles, we begin to see that we have a choice in the matter. We see the power of both God's thoughts and our own to shape our perceptions.

Experiencing this contrast can be a helpful step. The store owner in the example above did this. She knew that her dark perception of her landlord caused her distress. She also experienced the bright view of people that miracles gave her. In the end, she was able to apply the new, miracle-inspired perspective to her landlord.

Now, if the store owner were to wake up the next day and start getting annoyed at her customers, it wouldn't cancel out the work she had done the previous day. It would simply give her more evidence of the power of her perceptions. The contrast between one day's view and the next would highlight the importance of her thoughts.

In my experience, many of us move in a zig-zag pattern as we go forward. We switch back and forth between our old views and God's inspired vision. This isn't necessarily a bad thing. In fact, this type of movement can assist us. The contrast helps us to become increasingly clear about the two ways of seeing.

If we wish, we can intentionally spend a few minutes rotating between our normal way of seeing and God's bright vision. Our way of seeing tends to make us feel alone and apart. God's vision opens our hearts to feelings of expansion and peace. If we rotate between these two types of vision, we'll begin to get a clear sense of the emotional difference between the two. This can give us a motivational boost to move forward.

Simplification

The three exercises that I presented in this chapter are very basic. However, the process of accepting a miracle – an experience of God's love – can be even simpler. I support everyone in finding a form that is personally meaningful.

A woman, for example, may be going through a difficult time in her life. She may turn to God and say, "God, things look pretty bleak. However, I'm open to a new view of this." That may be enough of a "process" for this person to open her mind to the inner healing of a miracle.

Another person may simply say, "God, I need a miracle," and in that moment, open his mind to the inflow of God's love. That's enough of a process as well, if it gives the person a sense of comfort and peace.

I find that sometimes I need a brief call to God, and other times I need to spend a long time outlining my personal thoughts and expressing a willingness to have them be replaced. Quite often I need some help from a friend in this process. I feel that it's important to stay flexible on the approach.

If we are feeling emotionally upset, we may want to add some structure to this practice. We can take one minute every quarter-hour and turn to God for miracles. Even if we're in a panic, we can panic for fourteen minutes and open to God for one full minute. In my experience, repeatedly offering God a minute every quarter-hour can produce very practical results.

Incidentally, the Workbook of *A Course in Miracles* is designed to build this type of habit. I always encourage those who are interested to practice the lessons in the Workbook. By the time a person has passed lesson 65 (out of 365), he or she is engaged in a habit of turning to God every hour, all day. In my opinion, there is no more valuable habit than this.

Summary

Let me restate a few basic points that I've covered in this chapter. A miracle, according to the Course, is an inner experience of God's love. To "accept a miracle" is to let our minds be healed, to accept God's inspired thoughts in place of our darkened ones.

Miracles produce a sense of peace, and they come freely into an open mind. They are blocked only when we choose to hold onto our old thoughts and perspectives.

I have focused, as the Course does, on the inner experience of a miracle. However, I don't mean to imply that miracles can't have remarkable outer results. The Course suggests that miracles can potentially heal and resolve problems of any sort.

However, the Course emphasizes that it is the inner shift – toward peace, clarity, gentleness – that we should focus on. Anything that happens because of that shift is a lovely after-effect of the miracle. If we focus on the outer results of a miracle, we may lose sight of the inner healing – the miracle itself.

In my practice, I try to aim for a calm sense of assurance that things are in God's hands. Once that happens (and sometimes it takes a long time to get to that point), I try to release the outer details of the situation to God.

Sometimes those outer details are changed in unusual ways. Other times there doesn't seem to be much of a change at all. Either way, I try not to be too concerned with the external results. Instead, I try to maintain a calm sense of assurance that God has taken over the problem.

The Course encourages us to aim for peace of mind. If a specific answer for a problem arises from that peace, that is wonderful. If we are simply left with a calm sense of comfort – that too is wonderful.

An important gauge is how we feel. If we are filled with a sense of peace and kindness, we can be sure that we have received miracles. If we remain in conflict or distress, we may not have received – or we may have lost sight of – the miracle. In that case, we can gently but firmly return to our practice of exchanging our thoughts for the comforting peace of God.

Two

Relationships

When I began working with *A Course in Miracles*, I was surprised to find that many of the Course's themes were familiar. Little of what the Course says is brand-new.

However, there *are* aspects of the Course that are rather unique. If I had to choose one of the most unique aspects, it would be the Course's emphasis on relationships.

According to the Course, the relationships we have with people are of immense value. They are actually pathways to the experience of God. The Course doesn't want us to seek God by ourselves up on a mountaintop. It wants us to look around, and find the light of God in everyone.

Many of us do place value on the "close" relationships in our lives – relationships that we have with our friends and family. But the Course highlights the importance of every encounter we have with anyone.

A smile from a stranger on the street can help us to feel spiritually connected. A kind word from someone in passing can give us a sense of peace. The Course emphasizes how powerful these brief moments of relationship can be. We have opportunities to reconnect with the presence of God everywhere.

When I began working with the Course, I made a mistake in this regard. At the time, I was reading books about the value of solitude. I blended together these books with the Course and decided that I was supposed to set off on a solitary "search for God." Needless to say, I didn't get very far.

I spent months by myself in this search. Every day I prayed, took walks in nature, read spiritual books – and gradually descended into a state of misery. It was baffling. Things weren't working, but I had no idea what I was doing wrong.

Looking back, the problem seems clear. I had decided that I didn't need other people – that the real deal was between me and God. This was an unfortunate mistake. In separating myself from other people, I cut myself off from what I was really seeking.

The turning point came when I began to realize that the phone calls from my family and the visits from old friends were the things that were *really* helping me to move forward. Ten minutes with a friend brought me more inner peace and spiritual connection than ten hours of my solitary quest.

I gradually began to realize that God wasn't "out there," a hidden treasure to be tracked down. God was in my brothers and my parents, and in the kind people in the grocery store. Once I began to see that, I took the Course's emphasis on relationships much more seriously.

Of course, I don't think that spending time by oneself is a bad thing. I also don't think that simply being around a lot of people is the answer.

The real issue, I feel, is our inner attitudes. How do we see the people in our lives? Do we see them as children of God or irritating bothers? Do we see people as bridges to the experience of God's love, or blocks to our peace?

According to the Course, God is within everyone we meet. Every moment of relationship offers us a chance to feel spiritually connected. As we find God's presence in those around us, we will feel God's presence more fully within ourselves.

Seeing Is Strengthening

One of the Course's central ideas about relationships is this: whatever we choose to *see* in other people, we will strengthen in ourselves. Whatever we *look for* in others, we will find within ourselves.

This is very different from the world's normal way of thinking. In a way, it's the opposite.

To illustrate this idea, let's imagine a school teacher. This teacher feels that the best way to teach his students is to point out their mistakes, so he can correct them. This is how the teacher himself was taught. It seems like the normal thing to do.

The problem with this approach, however, is that the more the teacher focuses on the mistakes in his students, the more he *sees* those mistakes. The teacher begins to see mistakes increasingly, even in his "good" students. He finds those same mistakes in everyone around him, as well. Before long, the teacher seems to be surrounded by error.

Thankfully, he can reverse this process. The teacher can begin to focus on the core goodness and intelligence in his students. Of course, he will still help his students with specific problems, but the emphasis will be on bringing out their innate good rather than squashing the bad.

Gradually, that goodness will become more and more apparent to the teacher. He will see it increasingly in his students, and in other people around him. He will also begin to find that goodness in himself. That, in my opinion, is what the Course is recommending.

So how do we shift from one of these cycles to the other? As always, the answer is a miracle. The Course doesn't want us to make this shift by ourselves. We're not asked to "force out" a sense of kindness or patience using our own personal efforts. We're just asked to stop, recognize our position, and ask God for an inner healing – a miracle.

Let me illustrate this process using the teacher. Perhaps one day, in his quest to "correct" the mistakes in his students, this teacher crosses a threshold. He finds himself angrily berating a student.

Later that day, he argues with an "irrational" school administrator. At home, he finds that his own children are exhibiting the same poor behavior as his students. He feels surrounded by "crazy people." He is overwhelmed.

That night, in a moment of open-mindedness, the teacher begins to consider the idea that there may be a new way to perceive things. "God," he says, "I see craziness everywhere. Even in my own kids. But I'm willing to receive a miracle. Please help me here."

The teacher then quietly sits for a few minutes, offering his thoughts to God in exchange for a miracle. His mind opens, and he begins to feel calm – calmer than he has all day.

After a few moments, a memory comes to his mind of a kindness that one student exhibited toward another that day. "I forgot about that," the teacher says to himself. "I tend to overlook those little acts of kindness."

Another memory comes to mind – of a student who had to leave school to attend to family problems at home. "These kids are under a lot of pressure, more than I was at their age," he thinks.

The teacher's heart begins to open, compassionately, to his students. Finally, he thinks, "These kids deserve more support than I've been giving them," – and he's struck by that thought. It seems to come into his mind like an unexpected warm breeze.

After a few minutes, the teacher opens his eyes. He realizes that he has moved into a whole new perception of his students.

As he thinks about one student, then another, he sees gentle, wise qualities that he had never before acknowledged. He also, surprisingly, sees himself in a new light. Although he began the day feeling like a "failure" as an educator, he now sees great potential in himself to counsel and support his students. He feels grateful for the new perspective.

In that example, the turning point was the teacher's willingness to exchange his views for God's. The teacher didn't sit down and say, "I'm going to force myself to get a new attitude here." He simply turned, with an open mind, to God. He received God's benevolent thoughts.

An open mind, says the Course, is all that God needs. We are asked to become willing to exchange our thoughts for miracles. God will fill us with His loving thoughts, and this inner healing will, quite likely, transform our outer relationships as well.

It's remarkable how little time this inner healing needs. For the teacher, the exchange of his old perceptions for a new one may have required no more than a few minutes. The exchange simply awaited his willingness.

Miracles don't need a great deal of time to reach us. In a way, they are already here. What takes time is for us to open our minds to receive them. When we do become open, though, God can work quickly.

The Work

A Course in Miracles offers many insights on opening to the experience of a miracle. I'd like to jump right to one of the most powerful tools in the whole Course.

As I wrote earlier, the Course says that miracles are waiting for us all the time. We can accept a miracle – an experience of God's love – at any moment. The primary blocks to miracles are our own darkened thoughts. By loosening our grasp on our old thoughts, we open our minds to miracles.

In this chapter, I'd like to add a few more ideas on this process. According to the Course, we often "store" our dark thoughts in the form of grievances toward people. Grievances (or resentments) are, in fact, among the most common "hiding" places for our dark thoughts.

To illustrate this idea, let's imagine our minds as being filled with rows of cubbyholes. Each cubbyhole represents a particular relationship in our lives. We have cubbyholes for our parents, our children, and our friends. We even have cubbyholes for people we haven't seen in years.

In each cubbyhole, we store various thoughts toward the particular person. Some of these cubbyholes contain largely benevolent thoughts. Others are filled with grievances and other dark thoughts.

We may think that everything is stored away neatly. After all, we rarely "look" into most of these compartments. However, the fact that we're not aware of our stored-away thoughts doesn't mean that they're not affecting us.

The Course asks us to open up each cubbyhole, and clean out any dark thoughts that we're storing inside. In doing this, we clear out the darkness from every corner of our minds.

As an example of this, I may have a row of cubbyholes that represent people whom I haven't seen in years. I may not think that it's important to identify my thoughts toward these people – after all, I may never see them again.

The Course, however, points out that my thoughts toward these people are still in my mind, and those thoughts may be blocking the full experience of a miracle. The Course asks me to open each cubbyhole, and let God flush out any dark thoughts I'm storing inside.

I may decide to "take a look" at my thoughts toward a handful of people whom I haven't seen in twenty years. As I begin to think of those people – and honestly identify my thoughts toward them – I may find a significant amount of resentment or anger stored away. As I give over those resentful thoughts to God, and let Him exchange my grievances for miracles, my overall sense of peace is increased.

The Course wants us to open up every cubbyhole – open every relationship to God. Although this process may seem overwhelming (after all, most of us have thousands of these "relationship cubbyholes"), I find that the practice forms a momentum. The first dozen, or hundred, compartments that we open may require a reasonable amount of effort. But then our minds become comfortable with the process, and things begin to flow more smoothly.

This, in my opinion, is one of the most powerful practices in the Course. By identifying and releasing the "stored grievances" in our minds, we create a wide opening for God's miracles to flow in. The practice requires honesty – even some courage. But the results can be felt in a very practical way. I often feel an increased sense of peace by allowing just one cubbyhole to be cleaned out by God.

To summarize, there are two main points that I'm building on in this chapter. The first is that our dark thoughts are the primary blocks to miracles. The second point is that grievances are among the most common forms of dark thoughts. As we open up our grievances to God, and let Him replace them with miracles, our minds are healed. This will be my focus for the current chapter.

Before moving on, I'd like to share an observation from my work with this type of practice. I occasionally find that there is some discomfort that arises when I first open a door on a locked-away relationship.

Someone may come to mind whom I haven't thought of in years – someone whom I have some grievances against. I immediately feel uncomfortable, and want to slam shut the door on that compartment. But if I take one more step, and say, "God, I have some dark thoughts toward this person. I didn't realize it until this moment, but I don't want to lock those thoughts away. Please take them, and replace them with your miracles," I am taking a powerful step.

The real challenge in this process is to turn the dark thoughts over to God instead of locking them back away in their cubbyhole. If we bury them away, says the Course, they won't suddenly be resolved. They will simply be hidden. If we want our minds to be healed, we need to give God permission to wash these thoughts away, and give us a new perception instead.

Having said that, I'd like to present an exercise that builds on these ideas. This exercise is one of the most challenging in this book. As I mentioned earlier, you're welcome to work with these exercises in whatever way is personally meaningful. I will, however, try to be as comprehensive in my presentation as possible.

Step 1. The first step in this process is to choose a person in your life who troubles you. It could be someone who seems quite irritating, or someone who seems just mildly annoying.

(ex. Debby, my co-worker.)

Step 2. Next, describe why this person troubles you, using as much detail as possible. You're encouraged not to "censor" your current perspective. This step calls for a great deal of honesty.

(ex. Debby constantly gossips, she always asks me to do things for her, and she acts very petty. I just don't like being around her. No one really likes being around her.)

Step 3. Even though these things may seem to be "facts" (and on the worldly level, some of them may be), let's reframe them in terms of our thoughts. Let's restate step two in the form of, "I'm choosing to see _____ (person) as _____ (quality)."

We may have some resistance to this. Part of our mind wants to say, "I'm not *choosing* to see things this way; they just *are* this way." Although things may indeed be this way on a behavioral level, the Course wants us to take responsibility for our thoughts about them.

Again, our job in this step is to rewrite each sentence from step two in the form, "I'm choosing to see _____ as _____." This is a powerful step because it involves taking full responsibility for our thoughts. By doing this, we're identifying the contents of the cubbyhole.

(ex. I'm choosing to see Debby as someone who constantly gossips, who always asks me to do things for her, and who acts very petty. I'm choosing to see Debby as someone I don't like being around. I'm choosing to see Debby as someone whom no one likes being around.)

Step 4. Now we can evaluate how we feel about what we're thinking. We're pulling these stored-away thoughts out into the light.

Let's ask ourselves: How do we feel about these thoughts? Are they bringing us peace? If not, might we be willing to accept a new set of loving thoughts and inspired perceptions?

If we find that we are willing to receive a new perception – a new set of thoughts for the cubbyhole – let's say the following prayer:

God, I lay these thoughts before you.
I have no idea how I should look at this person.
But I am willing to receive a new view.
I give you my thoughts in exchange for your vision.

Then let's sit for a full minute and exchange, to the best of our ability, our view of this person for something new. God can show us a spark of beauty in this person that we may have never before seen. In seeing this spark of beauty, we will strengthen it in ourselves.

This can be a very holy process. It can bring peace to our minds and gentleness to our hearts. Our goal in this minute is to let our personal thoughts about this person be replaced with God's loving thoughts about him or her.

Like we did in the earlier exercises, we can use imagery in this practice. We can, for example, imagine this person stepping out from behind a costume. The costume is the old way we've been seeing her. But that isn't who she really is. We can envision this person shedding her old role like an actor at the end of a play, and coming forward to greet us.

Regardless of whether or not we use imagery in this process, our goal is to let a spark of God's light be revealed in this person. We want to exchange our old ways of seeing her for God's new way. Every time we do this with anyone in our lives, we're letting our own minds be healed.

In the Course, this type of exercise holds a central place. According to the Course, we can't find a real sense of peace if we're storing dark thoughts toward anyone. The Course teaches that there is an exact relationship between holding resentments and feeling unhappy. Every dark thought that we hold toward anyone causes us pain.

When I first read this idea in the Course, I was stunned. My dark thoughts toward that slow driver on the road are causing me pain? My judgmental thoughts toward those people on television have an impact on *me*? The Course says yes. But it also says that if I let God show me a spark of innocence in those people, I'm doing the best thing for my own state of mind.

That is why it can be so valuable to identify our current thoughts about a person, and become willing to exchange those thoughts for miracles – God's loving thoughts. As we do this, our own minds are healed.

If we do indeed take a minute to trade our thoughts for miracles, there are a couple things that can happen. We may begin to feel a lightening of our hearts, or we may feel stuck in our old perceptions.

If we feel stuck, it doesn't mean that we've failed. The simple act of practicing strengthens our desire for a change. It is a statement of willingness to let God step in. If we hold our focus – regardless of immediate results – we may find changes in our perspective slipping in over time.

As always, a sense of peace is an indication that we're on the right track. God's miracles bring peace to our minds and lighten our hearts. That is what we're aiming for.

In the example that I gave above, the person admitted that she held a negative view of her co-worker Debby. If this person is indeed willing to exchange her thoughts for miracles, she may find a warm sense of appreciation coming to fill her heart. She may see qualities in her co-worker that she had overlooked before.

Regardless of how the miracle transforms her perceptions, she will end up feeling more peaceful than before. In letting God heal her view of another person, she is letting her own mind be healed.

To Forgive Divine

Forgiveness is a major theme in the Course. It is the basis of the exercise I just presented, and of the next couple as well. Forgiveness is so central to the Course that one could say that *A Course in Miracles* is really a course in forgiveness.

To be clear, though, the Course uses the word "forgiveness" in a different way than we're used to. I'd like to touch on the Course's definition of the word before going any further.

When the Course talks about forgiveness, it's talking about the process of letting God heal our minds – letting God clean out the cubbyholes. Forgiveness isn't something that we do by ourselves. Forgiveness, as the Course uses the word, is a God-given inner healing.

The Course is clear that we don't need to "push out" forgiveness using our own efforts. We don't need to "force ourselves" to feel charitable toward a person. All that we need do is allow God to give us a miracle – an inner healing, a replacement for our current view.

It took me a long time to understand this. For a long time, I'd get to a point of clarity about my negative thoughts and say, "Wow. I have a lot of dark thoughts toward this person. I better change them into loving thoughts." I'd then sit down and try to alter my thinking.

The problem was that I tried to do this all by myself. It was an enormous struggle. I felt as though I was locked in a battle between one part of my mind and another. I felt that there was a "war" to be won – that I had to personally conquer my dark thoughts with kind ones.

As you can imagine, I didn't have a great deal of success. Then, one day, I realized that I was misunderstanding things. The Course was asking us to let *God* orchestrate this work. It wasn't me who had to direct the healing process; all I had to do was allow God to step in.

Suddenly, things became a bit easier. When I found myself angry at someone, I didn't try to fight my anger. Instead, I said, "God, here it is. Here are my thoughts and feelings about this person. I'm really angry right now. But I'm willing to let you heal my mind. I'm willing to accept a miracle." I didn't have to manufacture healing; I simply had to open to it. This approach worked much better.

The Course repeatedly emphasizes that healing (or forgiveness) is of God. We do not "make" healing happen. All we can do is clear the way for it. It is God who replaces our dark thoughts with His loving ones. It is God who effects this exchange. Our willing, active cooperation in this process is certainly required. But we are participants, not directors of it.

Before continuing, I'd like to address another idea about forgiveness that may seem like a side note. However, it's such a common misperception that I feel it's important to discuss.

Although the Course stresses the importance of practicing forgiveness – exchanging our dark thoughts about people for God's miracles – it is *not* suggesting that we should become doormats in the process. The Course wants us to be as respectful to ourselves as to others. To "forgive" someone doesn't mean that we should suffer through any form of mistreatment.

This is a common association. Many of us think, "This person acts nasty to me. If I forgive him, I'll have to suffer through more nastiness. If I don't forgive him, at least I'll be safe." The implication is that forgiveness means submitting to abuse. It does not.

Forgiveness, in the Course's use of the word, means, "With God's help, I'm going to relieve my mind of the pain of carrying around my dark thoughts. I'm going to ask for help in seeing this person through God's eyes." That's all. It doesn't mean that we are to stay with a physically abusive spouse, or jump through hoops for a manipulative friend.

Forgiveness is concerned with the healing of our minds. While this process is unfolding, we're asked to treat ourselves with kindness and respect. We're asked to show ourselves the same gentle care that a loving parent would show toward a child.

Of course, there may come a day when we're genuinely unbothered by behavior that used to feel hurtful. But that day will come in its own time.

For now, we're asked to be gentle and kind with ourselves as we honestly and bravely offer up our dark thoughts to God. Forgiveness does not ask that we tolerate – or mask – a sense of pain along the way.

Closer to Home

Having said that, the Course *does* ask us to be extremely clear about our part in the process. If there is a difficult relationship in our lives, it's very unlikely that all the dark thoughts are coming from the other person.

In some cases, the other person may be in a state of irrationality. We're not asked to submit to inappropriate behavior on his or her part. But we are asked to take responsibility for our side of things, and offer any unpeaceful thoughts to God.

We may find, to our chagrin, that we have more dark thoughts in the cubbyhole than we suspected. This may be discomfiting, but it's actually a very positive step.

The Course wants us to be honest with ourselves about our dark thoughts. The miracle will replace those dark thoughts and lead us in the direction of peace. However, we have to be honest about where we currently are.

This isn't always an easy process. Few of us want to acknowledge our dark thoughts. Most of us don't even want to *think* about acknowledging our dark thoughts. But the Course encourages this clean-up work. It asks us to identify our blocks, and immediately hand them over to God to be removed.

Let me illustrate this process using a simple example. Let's imagine that a friend of mine schedules a get-together with me and then doesn't show up. I feel angry and a bit hurt. I may be tempted to cover these feelings up — to say, for example, "Oh well, I don't care about being stood up." That isn't what the Course wants us to do.

If I'm feeling angry or hurt, and I simply cover up those feelings, I'm actually locking the problem away from God. Covering up my feelings may seem to resolve things for a short while, but the bad feelings will remain. I may find myself still upset about the event months or years later.

Does this mean that I should "express my anger" instead? Definitely not, if "expressing my anger" means that I attack the other person. To blame someone else for our state of mind isn't healing.

The Course suggests that we take a rather challenging two-step move. We are asked to come out of denial about our dark thoughts, and then immediately offer those thoughts to God to be removed.

We may have to repeat this process for a while, and we may find ourselves faced with the temptation to sweep our darkness under a veil of denial, or fixate on the mistakes of other people. We're asked to sidestep both of those tendencies.

To illustrate this idea using the example above, let's say that I find myself feeling upset about being stood up. Instead of covering up my feelings – or pinning them on the other person – I bring my sense of anger to God.

I say, "God, I feel angry about being stood up. I think that this person doesn't care about our friendship. I feel mistreated right now. Those are my thoughts and feelings, as honestly as I can state them. I offer them to you. Please give me a sense of peace."

If I am indeed able to place my thoughts and feelings in God's hands, and open to a miracle, I might find that my whole perspective on the situation is altered. Either way, the focus is on bringing my dark thoughts to God. Regardless of what happens on the outer level, this inner healing will bring me peace.

Although this is simple in theory, it can be a challenging practice. It requires honesty and effort. I am no expert at it. However, the Course doesn't ask us to be perfect – it simply asks us to practice.

The process of bringing our dark thoughts to God is actually a great gift to ourselves. We cast our burden before

God – the burden of our anger, our fear, our sense of hurt. We don't hide these things from God. Rather, we bravely offer them up to Him. As we bring our dark thoughts to God, He exchanges them for His healing miracles.

Neutrality

Some people read the Course's ideas about relationships and say, "Hey, this stuff is a little dark – all this talk about identifying grievances and dark thoughts and so forth. I thought *A Course in Miracles* was just about being kind and loving."

The Course is definitely about being kind and loving. But the Course wants us to unblock our minds to the flow of God's great kindness. The Course asks us to release our inner blocks so that God's love can flow through us more freely.

Every time we let God heal our view of another person, we're letting an inner block be removed. Every time we choose to see a person in a negative light, we're adding a block to our minds. That is why the Course focuses so heavily on relationships. Every moment of relationship is a step forward or backward, depending on how we use it.

Let's say, for example, that I have a five-minute encounter with a person at work. I may not think that this encounter is very important. The Course, however, says that immense healing can come from the interaction. If I let miracles transform my view of this person in the five minutes that we're together, I'm allowing my mind to be healed. That five-minute healing will stay with me.

Building on this idea, I'd like to present a variation of the exercise we did above. I find these types of exercises to be extremely powerful. If we do them correctly, we allow a relationship to be transformed – and in the process, allow our minds to be healed. Every time we identify a dark thought in a cubbyhole and allow it to be replaced with a miracle, we're taking a step toward peace.

This version of the exercise may require more honesty than the last one. In the first relationship exercise, we chose someone who irritated us. It may have been easy to identify our thoughts about the person – some of them may have been emotionally charged. In this exercise, we'll choose someone who seems "neutral." This one may require a little more looking.

As a preface, the Course points out that we can let our view of *anyone* be transformed. We can do some work with every relationship in our lives – even apparently "neutral" ones. As we let any relationship be healed by God, we'll feel a greater sense of inner peace.

Step 1. Let's begin by choosing someone who is a rather "neutral" person. This should be someone who doesn't bother you very much, but who doesn't cause you joy either. It's best to choose someone whom you know reasonably well.

(ex. My child's teacher, Ms. Hewlett.)

Step 2. How do you see this person? Feel free to describe both the "positive" and "negative" qualities you see in him or her. You can use the "I see _____ (person) as _____ (quality)" format.

(ex. Well, I see Ms. Hewlett as very attentive, but also a bit uptight. I see her as somewhat immature on the emotional level. I do see her as a very capable teacher, though. I see her as an OK person.)

Step 3. When we look at our perceptions of "neutral" people, we'll often find that we have various kind thoughts offset by various unkind thoughts. We'll often find critical thoughts offset by appreciative ones. All of our thoughts taken together "grey out" into a "neutral" perception.

The Course is asking us to give over our whole batch of thoughts and perceptions to God, in exchange for something more pure. We may not think that this individual is a significant person in our lives. However, the Course sees the relationship as very important. This person is both a mirror for our dark thoughts and a bridge to the experience of God.

Recognizing the importance of healing our perceptions of this person, let's say:

God, I have laid out my thoughts about this person.
I now ask for a clearer way of seeing him/her.
Please take my perceptions and replace them with yours.
How would you have me see this person?

Then let's rest in a state of open-mindedness for a full minute, and feel ourselves exchanging our views of this person for God's view. All that we need to do is open the door to God – to express our willingness to adopt a new, inspired view.

We'll know that we're doing this exercise correctly if we begin to see this person not as neutral, but as lovely – as a child of God.

The Course teaches that as our view of this person changes, our view of ourselves will change as well. We will begin to see ourselves in a more benevolent light. We will begin to feel an increased sense of God's love.

The Course makes the important point that our grievances – our dark thoughts – are the primary blocks to God's love. As we release our grievances, we automatically reconnect our minds and hearts with God. If we want to experience more love in our lives, we simply need to unblock the inner channel to it.

Even a handful of dark thoughts that we store toward a "neutral" person can cause some interference to the experience of God's love. As we exchange those dark thoughts for miracles, we will be comforted.

Let me touch on the example that I gave above. In the example, the parent found that she harbored a mix of thoughts toward her child's teacher. Some were peace-producing thoughts. Other thoughts produced a sense of irritation.

For example, when the teacher behaved attentively (in the parent's view), the parent was happy. When the teacher acted in an emotionally immature way, the parent was upset. These behaviors seemed fairly balanced, in the parent's view – thus producing an overall sense of "neutrality."

The Course is asking us to realize that we can trade these "neutral" views for a miracle. We're asked to go beyond the whole lot of these perceptions, and let our minds be truly healed.

The miracle will so alter our vision that we'll see a spark of beauty beyond the "good" and "bad" human qualities. As we see this spark in others, we will strengthen it in ourselves. Eventually, we'll find that God's light is present within this previously "neutral" person. Once that happens, we will never see the person in the old way again.

Friends and Family

Let's take this exercise to the next logical step. In the first version of this exercise, we chose someone who irritated us. Then we chose someone who seemed "neutral." Now let's choose someone whom we really love.

Again, our goal is to let our perceptions be so cleansed that we see the light of God in all these people. As we see God's light in another person, God's light is strengthened in us.

Step 1. To begin, choose someone who is a close friend or family member of yours.

(ex. My husband Michael.)

Step 2. Next, describe how you see this person – at his or her "best" and "worst."

(ex. I see Michael as a really sweet guy. I really love him a lot. He does get a bit short-tempered at times, but that doesn't bother me. I see him as really kind and sensitive almost all the time.)

Step 3. The Course suggests that even when we see our close friends and family members at their "best," we're seeing only a small approximation of their true worth and beauty. Let's become willing to exchange our benevolent perceptions for an even lovelier one. Let's say:

> *God, I do indeed feel a great deal of love toward this person.*
> *However, I am willing to see an even greater beauty in him/her.*
> *Please replace my views with yours.*
> *Show me how you see this one.*

This can be a very holy experience. A person who was a friend can be revealed as the very light of God. We may be rendered speechless by the beauty we see in him or her. That vision is the gift of a miracle.

In time, says the Course, we will learn to see the light of God in everyone. Practicing with those whom we already see in a loving way can give us a helpful boost in this regard.

As we learn to see God's beauty in those who are "close" to us, we may find ourselves able to transfer that vision to those who are "distant" or troublesome. We'll eventually learn to apply this vision indiscriminately, and thus heal every corner of our minds.

Acceptance

I'd like to address a piece of conventional wisdom that varies somewhat from the Course's approach.

According to conventional wisdom, we should try to accept the people in our lives. In other words, we shouldn't try to "fix" people, but accept them as they are.

The Course agrees with this idea, but it means something very unique by the word "acceptance."

To illustrate what I mean, let's imagine that I have a roommate. This roommate leaves his clothes strewn around our apartment, and never cleans his dishes. This causes me great annoyance. I try to convince my roommate that he needs to change – to straighten up around the house and pitch in more – but my efforts go nowhere.

I try to change him for years. Then, one day, I say, "I give up. I just have to accept my roommate as he is."

What I mean by that is, "This guy is just a lazy person. He's not going to change."

Although that's probably a slight step forward – it may be better than engaging in constant battles with my roommate – it's not what the Course means by acceptance. When the Course asks us to accept someone as he is, it means accept him as he *really* is – in God's view.

God can direct my vision past my roommate's body, past his behavior, and even past his current attitudes to the spiritual magnificence that lies beyond. That is what the Course means by acceptance. Of course, this process clearly requires a miracle.

Let's imagine that my roommate is bothering me one day. Instead of washing my hands of his "laziness," I decide to turn to God for a miracle – an inner healing.

I say, "God, this guy really bothers me. I see him as lazy, insensitive, and selfish. Those are my perceptions. But I want to see something else in him – something which even *he* may not be aware of. Help me to accept him as he really is."

Then I sit for a minute or two, exchanging my views for God's. With God's help, I begin to see little bits of kindness and innocence in my roommate that I hadn't seen before. I let those bits of kindness grow until they become all I see of him. A feeling of peace comes over me. "Thank you for this vision," I say. "This I can accept."

I may still ask my roommate to contribute around the house, but most likely the resentment behind those requests will be gone. I have accepted a new vision of my roommate. This true acceptance will benefit *me*.

My roommate may not see himself in this new, miracle-inspired way. But if I hold the vision, he might find himself sharing it, and his behavior might begin to reflect that greater sense of worth. Either way, my mind is healed. I have let a miracle touch me.

An important point is that the Course asks us to look past a person's body, behavior, and current state of mind. Typically, those are the only things that we *do* focus on. But the Course stresses how important it is to let our vision be guided beyond.

Another way to describe this process is that we're being asked to align our perceptions with God's. God, says the Course, sees us as beloved children of His. We generally see ourselves otherwise.

We see that person as rude, this one as desirable, and so forth. But our views are based on our perceptions of bodies, behavior, and personalities. God can refocus our vision past those things, to the spirit beyond.

Is this process easy? For part of our minds, it's as easy as returning home after a long and tiresome journey. But for the other part of our minds – the part that is often most dominant – it is very difficult.

We may find it challenging to look past a person's attitudes. We may feel outraged at the idea that the presence of God is hidden somewhere within this person. The Course says that we have spent most of our lives denying this presence. It may take some time before we become comfortable with the new perception.

As I've tried to clarify, I am no expert at this. Like many of us, I am prone to periods of resentment. I sometimes find myself stuck on a dark perception until I am joined by someone who will help – someone who will accept a miracle with me.

The Course encourages cooperation in this endeavor. If we can help a friend with this process, or accept help from a friend, we are joining in a very powerful partnership.

Going Together

In order to keep things practical, I'd like to present one last summary exercise. This one doesn't require any writing. I will, however, include a sample response as an example.

Step 1. To begin, think of someone in your life – it could be anyone.

(ex. My employee Thomas.)

Step 2. Next, review to yourself how you see this person. Include his or her personality quirks, appearance, positive and negative qualities, and so forth.

(ex. Thomas is a nice guy I suppose. He's a pretty sharp dresser. A bit low-key, but nice. Reasonably good worker.)

Step 3. Let's now remind ourselves that these perceptions have nothing to do with who this person really is. They are, in fact, a substitute for the clearer perception of a miracle. Let's say:

God, I have no idea how to look at this person.
Lead my vision to what you see.

Then let's do as we did earlier. Let's relinquish all the images and ideas we have about this person, and see him as though we know nothing about him. Let's allow God's vision of him to replace our old way of seeing.

If we're doing this with an open mind, we'll be surprised at the spark of loveliness we're beginning to see in this person.

Step 4. If we are able to begin to find some light in this person that we didn't see before, let's now run through the same process with ourselves. Let's say:

God, I have no idea how to look at myself, either.
Show me how you see me.

And then let's allow that same inspired vision to reveal us to ourselves in a new light. We may want to rotate between the other person and ourselves, realizing that what we choose to see in one of us will become more apparent in both.

This, again, is one of the most fundamental ideas in *A Course in Miracles*. What we see in anyone, we strengthen in everyone. The wonderful thing about this idea – and about the Course's approach in general – is that we can use it very broadly.

We can walk down the main street of whatever town we live in, and find countless opportunities to elevate our vision. A person walks by. We acknowledge our current perception of her, and then ask God for a substitute. A spark of holiness begins to twinkle in her. We feel this same spark in ourselves.

That is a key practice of the Course. It does take some work to practice adopting God's inspired vision. But the opportunities are limitless.

God will help us see that the people behind the store counter aren't servants; they are unrecognized saints. The patients in a doctor's office aren't sick bodies; they are angels seeking help.

As we allow God to reveal His presence in those around us, we will find, increasingly, that we are in touch with that same presence in ourselves. That is what the Course means by healing.

Practical Application

The Course's ideas can sometimes feel a bit lofty. However, they can be used in very practical, down-to-earth ways. Let me offer a few examples to illustrate.

Let's imagine that I need to complete a business project – a project that will require some clarity of thought. Unfortunately, I'm not feeling very clear-minded on this day. In fact, I'm feeling quite cloudy.

At this point, I may turn to God and simply say, "God, I'm feeling cloudy; please give me some clarity." If my mind is truly open to that exchange, it may be enough to lift me into a higher place.

However, let's imagine that I need an extra boost. Drawing on the Course's idea of seeing-as-strengthening, I may wish to try a little exercise.

I begin by reminding myself that whatever I perceive in others, I reinforce in myself. Building on that idea, I choose to think of someone I know who seems like a clear-minded person.

I hold this person in mind, focusing on the clarity I see in her. Then I say, "God, please show me this person's clarity even more. All I want to see in her is your wisdom."

I sit for a minute and allow God to expand my view of this person. As I let God show me the clarity and wisdom in *her*, I'm simultaneously increasing the clarity and wisdom in myself.

Of course, the person I'm thinking of doesn't have to be physically present. My view of her is in my mind. As God replaces my view with His vision, my own mind is changed.

One could try an "advanced" version of this same exercise. Let's imagine, for example, that a woman wishes to increase her capacity to be generous. This woman sits down and begins to think of the most *ungenerous* people in her life – various tight-fisted misers.

She turns to God and says, "God, I am willing to be shown the generous spirit in these people. I can't for the life of me see it myself, but I trust that you can show it to me."

Then this woman releases the perceptions that she currently holds of these people. She lets the images of their stinginess be swept away by a miracle.

She gradually, with God's help, begins to "see" a potential for giving in each one of these people. In fact, she recalls a handful of incidents in which these people were generous to some degree. She lets those sparks of generosity grow in her mind, until they become all she sees.

This type of process will not only heal the woman's view of these people; it will actually sweep away her own ungenerous thoughts.

The woman will likely find, at the conclusion of this exercise, that her own capacity to be generous has increased. In letting God clear away her ungenerous perceptions of others, her own mind has been lifted into a state of generosity.

The problem is that we often do this in reverse. Let's imagine a business manager who sees his staff as lazy. Every time that this manager finds a new laziness – and locks it into place as a "quality" of a staff member – he's filling his own mind with thoughts of laziness.

The Course reminds us that thoughts have an effect on whoever holds them. Fixating on other people's faults is like throwing some mud on our own car's windshield. It obstructs *our* vision.

This business manager's staff may indeed be exhibiting lazy behavior. Perhaps everyone will agree with him on this. However, the manager needs to be primarily concerned with his own state of mind.

If he turns to God and says, "God, help me to see some spark of inspiration in these people," he may glimpse a potential for greatness in his staff members. He may, in fact, find a way to bring out that potential.

Whether or not the staff end up changing their behavior, the manager's mind is changed by this process. Every time he accepts a miracle instead of a grievance, he is allowing some mud to be cleaned from his windshield.

This process can be used to heal a sense of failure, as well. Let's say that I am ashamed of a mistake I made several years ago. Perhaps I had the opportunity to embark on an interesting career path, but I was frightened at the time and sabotaged myself. Ever since that point, I've felt bad about the event. The Course's ideas on relationships can help me to move forward.

I can turn to God and say, "God, I feel terrible about what happened. I feel that I really messed up. But I want to release my sense of guilt to you. I know that you can set things right."

Then, as a support to that prayer, I think of someone who is in a similar situation. I think, for example, of a friend of mine who passed up a similar career opportunity and feels regret about her decision.

I hold that person in mind and say, "God, show me this person's innocence. I want to see her as completely forgiven, absolved of any consequences of her mistake."

I may find that it's easy to let God sweep away this friend's mistake, in my perception. I may find that I can easily see my friend as deserving of a second chance, and a third – as many as she needs.

It may be easy for me to perceive God's abundant love and care for my friend. As I let my mind become filled with the vision of my friend's innocence, I may find this vision extending to my own situation as well.

The Course asks us to take every relationship very seriously. Each one can move us (and potentially the other person) forward or backward, depending on the thoughts we extend. Even if a person is not physically present, our thoughts about him or her are powerful.

In "intimate" relationships, in which there is a great degree of interaction, our movements forward and backward can be accelerated. However, the Course doesn't want us to look at one relationship as important and another as meaningless. Any thought that we extend toward anyone will affect us.

The Course is trying to teach us the importance of every thought we hold – and every relationship we have. Though it may be difficult to see, our view of the people on the street will influence our view of our family and of ourselves.

If we let God show us a spark of beauty in a stranger, we may find ourselves seeing that same spark in our spouse and children – and in ourselves.

Summary

The Course spends a great deal of time discussing the importance of relationships. I have touched on only a small segment of the Course's ideas in this chapter.

One idea that I haven't covered in detail – but will point out – is that as we release another person from our narrow perceptions, we'll often find ourselves overcome with a sense of tenderness toward him or her.

We may then find ourselves entering into a new, inspired relationship with the person. This new relationship can serve as a wonderful vehicle on the path to God.

The Course teaches that this can happen in an instant, even with someone whom we just met. It can also happen after many years of turmoil in a tight-knit relationship.

The outer form of a relationship doesn't impede God's ability to heal it. The only thing that impedes it is our old perceptions of it.

That is why the Course is constantly asking us to be clear about our thoughts. We're asked to take responsibility for our perceptions of other people (and ourselves), and offer those perceptions to God in exchange for a miracle.

As we trade our old vision, like a worn-out pair of eyeglasses, for His, we will find ourselves perceiving a spark of holiness in those around us. This spark can then grow, in our view of both others and ourselves.

Three

Inner Guidance

Some people read the ideas in *A Course in Miracles* and say, "Sure — inner peace, seeing sparks of holiness. Sounds great. But how about practical things? What am I supposed to do about my job situation? What should I say to my kids when they're acting up?"

These are good questions. It's true that the Course doesn't give us a formula for choosing the right job. It doesn't tell us what exact decisions we should make in our lives. Clearly, it would be impossible for a book to give such precise instructions to everyone.

Thankfully, though, we have help. The Course says that we can turn to God for guidance on any decision before us — no matter how "big" or "small" it seems to be.

God is available to guide us at every moment. He doesn't get bored or tired of helping us.

Seeking God's guidance on our decisions isn't a mysterious practice. It just means that we try to reach beyond our own personal perspectives when deciding what to do. We admit that we don't have the answer, and say, "God, please give me some direction." Then we open our minds to a prompting.

We can ask God for guidance on our business affairs, on our relationships, and on any other decisions. He will guide us, says the Course, if we turn to Him with an open mind.

In a way, asking for guidance is the same as receiving a miracle – or seeing a spark of holiness. In all three of these practices, we exchange our own thoughts and perspectives for God's vision. We clear a space in our minds for God's inspired thoughts to enter.

Before going any further, I'd like to clarify my use of a phrase. When I write about "receiving guidance," I use the term in a very broad way. Guidance may come in the form of a "nudge" to do something. We might feel "inspired" to take some action. God may speak to us through another person. We may find a thought or image entering our minds that gives us direction.

Florence Shinn, who wrote *The Game of Life and How to Play It*, talked about receiving guidance in this way:

The answer will come through intuition (or hunch); a chance remark from someone, or a passage in a book, etc., etc. The answers are sometimes quite startling in their exactness.

The key is for us to open our minds to the inflow of God's wisdom. As we do this, God will reach through whatever channels are open. It doesn't matter whether we receive guidance from a thought, a hunch, a vision – or through the wise words of a friend. As long as our minds are open, God's guidance will come.

The Course places a great deal of value on the practice of seeking God's guidance. Asking for guidance not only helps us with the decisions in our lives; it also helps us to feel spiritually connected. Even if we don't feel that we've "received" anything at first, the process of asking is an act of trust. It is a way of healing our sense of aloneness.

So how does the Course recommend that we seek God's guidance? The Course approaches the practice very broadly. The whole Workbook of the Course is designed to give us tools to open ourselves to God's direction. As I mentioned earlier, I encourage you to consult the Course itself for a full presentation. I'm happy to outline a few ideas, but they shouldn't be taken as a substitute for the Course's comprehensive approach.

Before I begin, I'd like to point out that the process of receiving God's guidance is, by its nature, a personal experience. The approaches and forms vary from person to person. I share this in order to clarify that my understanding is based largely on my own experiences to date. I encourage you to explore what works for you.

Removing Interference

Just as God is always offering us miracles, so is He always offering us direction. According to the Course, we don't have to beg God for guidance on our decisions; He is trying to guide us all the time. The only thing we need to do is remove our interference.

Our "interference" to receiving guidance takes many forms, including our personal plans, personal analyses of our situations, and so forth. Any thought that we're tightly holding onto is a potential block. As we begin to open our minds, realizing that we don't have the widest perspective on things, we gradually become open to God's promptings.

The Course is clear that we do need to quiet and open our minds in order to receive guidance. God will not force His wisdom over our thoughts. His guidance is as gentle as He is, and it merely waits for an opening.

There have been times that I've turned to God seeking guidance, and haven't received anything. But then, hours later – when my mind became quiet and open – I suddenly received an answer. It wasn't that God waited to help me. My mind simply wasn't open at first to receive that help.

To illustrate this point, let's imagine that I am faced with a deadline on a creative project. The deadline is looming, and I have several decisions to make. I need to make them quickly. I'm beginning to feel agitated.

I decide to turn to God for guidance. "God," I say, "please give me some direction. Give me a thought about what to do here. But hurry – the deadline is almost here."

I don't seem to receive anything, which only increases my agitation. "God, please help," I say. "I need some guidance here. Hurry up." Nothing comes to me. "God, I need some guidance – quickly." I don't receive anything.

If I keep asking from a state of agitation, I'll never hear the answer. I need to sit down and clear my mind for a minute. I need to create a space for God's guidance to enter. I have asked; He will answer. But I need to quiet things down. I'll never hear God's promptings if my mind is filled with my own agitated thoughts.

This places a good deal of responsibility on us. We're asked to clear an opening to receive God's guidance. We are the ones who are blocking it with our thoughts, and we are the ones who must release the blocks.

The process is similar to making an opening in a dam. God's guidance is like a river that we've dammed up. The river wants to enter; it is waiting at the edge of the dam. But we need to take down the blocks to it. Once we begin to clear a channel, the water can rush in.

Over the next few pages, I'll outline three common blocks to receiving guidance. I don't mean to suggest that these cover all the different forms of interference. However, I think they're a good starting point. After presenting them, I'll bring them together into a comprehensive exercise.

Releasing Perspectives

The first block I'd like to address is our tendency to hold onto our personal perspectives as we ask God for direction. As I covered in earlier chapters, our perspectives are very powerful. They color our whole experience. If we want to receive God's guidance, it's helpful to begin by releasing our own personal views of our situation.

Holding onto our own perspectives while asking for God's guidance is a partial exchange. It is like walking into a store and saying, "I'd like to trade my fifty cents for a warm drink." The store owner hands us the drink, but we merely tighten our grip on our coins.

"I'd like that drink," we say. The proprietor looks at us in puzzlement. The drink is right before us. However, we can't receive it unless we're willing to open our grasp — to give up our coins.

In a similar way, some of us outline the details of our problems to God as we ask for guidance, and then invest even tighter in those details. While this is understandable — especially when we're upset — it tends to block our experience of the answer.

God can't give us His direction if our minds are filled with our problems. There simply isn't any room. We need to let our old perspectives go, at least for a few moments, if we want to receive His insights.

It takes some discipline to take control of our thoughts and become willing to exchange them for God's guidance. I am certainly no expert at this. However, as with everything, the Course simply asks us to practice.

Let me present a simple exercise to illustrate this process. This will be a building block for a later, more comprehensive exercise.

Step 1. Here is a problem that I'm experiencing in my life:

(ex. My acting career is completely stalled.)

Step 2. Why is this a problem? Even if it seems "obvious" why it's a problem, feel free to describe your view here.

(ex. It's a problem because I'm going to run out of money in a few months if I don't get going. And there's a lot of competition for acting jobs. I need to get a few jobs under my belt if I want to stand out from the competition.)

Step 3. Next, let's consider the idea that our description of the problem – our perception of it – is a potential block to receiving God's guidance. This may sound strange, but sometimes our minds are so clouded with personal thoughts about the situation that there isn't room for anything else.

Let's try to let our perspectives go into God's hands – for at least a minute – and turn to Him with a completely open mind. Let's say:

> *God, here are my thoughts about my situation.*
> *I give them to you.*
> *Please exchange my thoughts for your wisdom.*
> *I am open to your guidance and direction.*

Then let's rest with an open mind for a full minute. While we're resting, let's continue to monitor our thoughts. If we find ourselves outlining the problem again, let's repeat the prayer and release our thoughts back to God.

In this minute, we're aiming for a calm, peaceful sense of assurance that God has taken the problem from us. Once that calm assurance comes over us, we may find that there are insights and thoughts of direction that follow. It's the sense of inner peace that we're aiming for, however. God's guidance will simply follow that peace.

As I've mentioned before, guidance can come to us in a variety of ways. We may turn over a problem to God, and find that we have a sense of peace about it. However, we don't immediately receive any insights about what to do.

Then, several hours later, a thought comes to mind that provides a solution. The fact that we didn't "get" an answer immediately didn't mean that we practiced incorrectly.

The fact that we received a sense of peace – a sense of assurance that God had taken the problem – meant that we did our job. As long as we kept that peaceful sense of assurance with us, the channel was open.

I feel that the goal in asking for guidance should always be a sense of peace and release. If we receive insights on a problem, but don't receive peace, we're not going to be much better off than before. The lack of peace may stay with us and create more problems.

However, when we do receive the gift of God's peace, our minds become clearer and more open. We can then receive insights, wisdom, and promptings more easily as we move forward.

Little Things

One practice that can help us open to God's guidance in our lives is the practice of asking for direction in "little" things.

As an example, let's imagine a man who is facing a difficulty in his business. This man is quite upset about his business situation, and his emotional distress is preventing him from recognizing God's guidance.

Although this man may be upset about his business problem, he may have no emotional charge around the question of where to eat lunch. Using that as an opening, he may want to begin by asking for God's guidance in this "little" area.

Is it really important where the man eats lunch? Perhaps not. But if the man turns to God for direction in this area, he may find himself inspired by the results. This can increase his comfort with the process of asking in wider contexts. Receiving God's help with a "little" area can calm the man's mind and boost his sense of trust.

Let me offer a personal example on asking for guidance in little things. I occasionally run errands, and try to stay open for direction while doing so. If I need to stop by a bookstore, for example, I may look for a prompting on which store to visit.

One day, a few years ago, I was driving down the street to mail a letter. As I passed a mailbox, I thought I spied a person whom I knew. I decided to park my car, say hello to the person, and mail my letter. However, I first "checked in" on the decision. I was fairly sure I would receive an OK on the matter.

To my surprise, I received a fairly strong sense to keep driving on to my normal post office. I was a bit stunned by this, as I rarely experienced a strong pull in decisions of this sort. However, I complied. I figured that perhaps the person I saw on the street wasn't the person I knew.

A few blocks from my post office, another reason appeared. I drove around a sharp curve, and there in the middle of the street was a little Beagle puppy.

I pulled to a stop and opened my door. Before I could even get out of my car, the puppy ran up to me and jumped onto my lap. He was delightfully happy, but he had no identification tags. He was obviously lost.

Not knowing what to do, I called the local police station on my car phone. I was directed to an animal specialist who explained that she knew exactly where this puppy lived – this was the second time he had escaped from his yard. She decided to take him back to his owners and have a talk with them about protecting him better.

In the end, the situation was resolved in a fine way. Perhaps the original "nudge" I received was a coincidence.

I really don't know. I do, however, think that God sees all our needs, and reaches through whatever channels are open to Him.

By increasingly placing our choices – even "little" ones – at God's disposal, we're offering Him more opportunities to lovingly guide us. We're also building our sense of trust in Him. The process helps both us and those we touch.

Before moving on, I'd like to address a couple ideas about the process of regularly asking for guidance. The first idea is that the Course doesn't ask us to become obsessive about the practice. We don't have to turn to God about every single choice that we make.

Clearly, if a child is about to run into traffic, we should stop him – not sit down and pray for guidance. The Course wants us to use common sense. However, when we do feel that we have an opening, we can seek God's help. He will direct us whenever we turn to Him with an open mind.

The second idea I'd like to share is that open-mindedness is, in my experience, essential. I have had little success in my attempts to seek guidance in a tight-fisted way. If I turn to God and say, "Tell me how to make money," I usually receive little direction. However, if I turn with an open heart and say, "Lead me where you would have me be," I'm often touched by the results.

The difference is the approach. If we approach God with an open mind and heart, we may indeed end up receiving guidance on money-making activities – inspiration to start a new business, or something of the sort. But if we do, it is because it's God's plan, not our own personal invention.

In its purest form, asking for guidance is an act of trust. What we're seeking, deep down, is an experience of being comforted and taken care of. That is what we really want. Ideally, we simply open our hearts to God and invite Him to lead us.

Asking for guidance is an act of commitment, and it requires us to become quiet and receptive. Later in this chapter, I'll discuss a few ideas about quieting our minds, as that can be an important practice. But I'd first like to briefly cover two other common forms of interference.

Personal Goals

In our culture, there is a great deal of emphasis placed on personal goals. Even as children, we're encouraged to outline our desires and "dream big." We're told to be clear about what we really want in life.

Although there is some freedom in that practice, it can also backfire on us. If we fixate too tightly on our personal visions of happiness, we run the risk of closing our minds to God's wider vision.

I share this because I have, at times, run myself into ruts pursuing personal goals. I've seen others do the same thing as well. We choose something we want, and then we doggedly chase after that thing. We keep chasing – perhaps for years – even though things aren't flowing very well.

Eventually, in a state of exhaustion, we sit down and say, "God, I really want this. Why aren't you helping me get it?" The answer may be that God has a better direction for us. Unfortunately, we never heard His guidance because we were fixated too tightly on our own goals.

As an illustration of this idea, let's imagine a woman who is an athlete. This woman has a goal of becoming an Olympic runner. She works hard at her training. She constantly reinforces her vision of winning a gold medal. Unfortunately, though, she never seems to get the right "breaks." Problems always prevent her from moving forward.

One day, feeling weary, she says, "God, you know I have this dream of winning a gold medal. I really want that. However, I'm willing to adopt a different goal if you would like. Please guide me in whatever way you wish."

That is a profound statement of open-mindedness. It is an act of faith. That open-mindedness will undoubtedly allow the woman to hear God's guidance more clearly. She may be guided in a new direction – or she may receive clearer guidance on attaining her original goal.

The point is that while the woman had her "nose to the grindstone," she risked missing out on God's gentle promptings. When she paused for a moment and asked God for direction, she opened her mind to hear. I feel that we, like her, need to loosen our grip on our personal goals – at least for a moment or two – and turn to God with a wide open mind.

We can be sure, says the Course, that God has our highest interests in mind. If He guides us toward something other than gold medals, it's because the new direction will give us greater joy. In allowing God to modify our direction, we're simply allowing Him to set our sights higher.

Plans

So far I've touched on a couple forms of interference: our personal perspectives, and personal goals. I'd like to look at one more form of interference: self-generated plans.

Many of us are taught to devise elaborate plans for our happiness. We're encouraged to set goals, and then make plans for reaching those goals. Although that works well on one level, it can also send us on wild goose chases.

I myself have spent a good deal of time setting goals, making plans to reach those goals, and actually attaining the goals. However, I often reached the end of that cycle, and realized that I wasn't any more peaceful or content than when I began. Even though I followed my plans, they didn't really lead me anywhere.

The Course understands this. It asks us to realize that we are like children – that we don't really know what's best for ourselves. But God does know, and He can direct our activities. Letting God guide us doesn't mean that we don't follow a plan. It's just that we don't invent this plan by ourselves.

I believe that God has a custom-tailored plan for each of us. This plan involves unique work in the world, specific relationships, and so forth. If we make a wrong turn, there is always a back-up plan; a re-route to get us back on track. We can never fall too far afield.

What we sometimes do, however, is strike off on our own. Whenever we say, "I have things handled, God – I know what to do," we risk closing our minds to God's guidance.

This doesn't mean that we're committing an irrevocable mistake. God will always steer us back on course. But it's like snapping shut a compass, saying, "I don't need this. I can make my way through these woods myself."

Why would we *want* to make our way through the woods by ourselves? We have an ever-present source of direction.

One common pitfall is to receive some guidance and then immediately shut the door. We may "get a piece of the plan," and then close our minds to the next step.

This can be a problem. It's like a quarterback getting one play from his coach, and then running that play over and over for the rest of the day. The play was simply one step of many; it was for a specific point in time. The quarterback has to keep his mind open to new instructions.

I find that, in order to receive God's guidance clearly, I have to continue to "check in." This doesn't mean that I sit around second-guessing old decisions. But if I currently feel stuck, I try to approach God with a clean slate. The plan for yesterday may not be the same as the plan for today.

I'd like to bring together these three types of interference into a composite exercise. When people say, "I just can't 'hear' anything from God – I can't get any guidance," I often suggest doing a comprehensive exercise like this one. It can help us create an opening in our minds to receive God's promptings.

Step 1. Here is an area of my life that is causing me some concern:

(ex. My job isn't fulfilling me, but I have no idea if I should look for something new.)

Step 2. Describe why this area of your life is causing you concern.

(ex. I don't want to get stuck in this job for another ten years. But I'm worried that if I look for something new, I might lose the financial security I have with my current job.)

Step 3. Describe what the ideal resolution of this situation would look like.

(ex. Ideally, I would find a new job that would have the same pay as my current job but be more fulfilling. Maybe a job that would give me some creative freedom.)

Step 4. Describe what you have done – or are planning to do – to improve this situation.

(ex. I did put together a resume and looked through some classified ads. But I didn't find anything. I'm planning to call up a few companies and ask them for interviews.)

Step 5. The Course now asks us to go one step further. It asks us to trade these perceptions, goals, and plans for God's direction. If we are willing to make this exchange, let's say:

> *God, I'm willing to give you these perspectives, goals,*
>   *and plans.*
> *Please give me your guidance instead.*
> *I don't know the best outcome, or how to attain it.*
> *But I trust that you do know, and will direct me.*

Then let's rest for a full minute, exchanging our thoughts for a sense of peace. If we find ourselves thinking about the problem in an anxiety-producing way, let's repeat the prayer (or one like it) and again release our thoughts to God. There may be quite a bit of back-and-forth that occurs in this process. As always, our goal is a sense of inner peace – a sense that God is here with us.

Once we begin to feel that sense of peace, we may find insights arising from that peace. If so, we may want to consider those as replacements for what we thought before. Our main goal in this exercise is to clean the slate of our old thoughts, goals, and plans. Once we clear an open space, God's wisdom can flow in.

As I mentioned earlier, if we receive nothing but a slight increase in peace during this practice, we're still on the right track. We can hold that direction and see what comes to us as we go along.

In the example above, the person very honestly outlined her thoughts, goals, and plans. Then she became willing to exchange them for God's guidance.

As she continues this process, she may receive insights that lead to unusual resolutions – for example, she may be inspired to volunteer with an organization that sets her on a new career path. Or she may be guided to set up a small business on the side. She may be prompted to speak with her boss about enriching the environment of her current company.

As I've mentioned, I feel that the essential step in asking for guidance is to release our personal thoughts, and open our minds to a broader view. Once we do that, God's guidance can reach us more easily. The specific guidance we need may come through a friend's comment, or it may come as an idea while we're sitting in traffic. The form is adaptable to our situation.

For best results, I feel that our focus should be on unblocking our minds. If we try to "grab hold" of specific insights, we may have some success. But if we gradually, diligently clear away our blocks to God, we'll create a wide opening. This will help us with both our current and future efforts to receive guidance.

Distinctions

Having discussed a few forms of interference, let me now turn to a question that is quite common.

Many times we'll feel that we have "received" something – a prompting, a nudge, an idea. However, we're not sure if it's inspired by God's wisdom, or if it's coming from our own personal thoughts. How do we tell the difference?

I feel that it's essential for each person to answer this question in a personally meaningful way. From the discussions I've had with people, there seem to be a vast number of discernment techniques.

Some people, for example, feel a "happy glow" around one choice, and an "empty feeling" around another choice. Other people talk about receiving one idea "from the head" and another "from the heart." Some feel a "pull" toward one direction rather than another. I believe that the process of discernment varies from person to person.

However, I would like to offer an important point on this matter from *A Course in Miracles*. The Course suggests that God's guidance will be peaceful, supportive, and respectful. It will not be critical, abusive, or controlling. We can use this as a "baseline" as we try to move in the right direction.

It may seem like common sense to say that God's guidance will be supportive rather than abusive. However, it's remarkable how many times people have said, "God is guiding me to hurt this person – it must be for the best." Or, "God wants me to do this thing, even though it will cause me pain." Those, I believe, are distorted perceptions of God's guidance.

The Course teaches that God's wisdom will help everyone it touches. That is why it is so different from our usual lines of thought.

Our ordinary "solutions" usually require someone to lose. We see ourselves as gaining at someone else's expense, or losing in order for him or her to be happy. God's guidance corrects our limited perceptions by offering a win-win solution for everyone.

Let me offer a couple of examples to illustrate what I mean. Let's imagine that I'm having a conflict with a client. I try to release my thoughts about the situation to God, and open to His guidance. I say, "God, I give you my thoughts and plans. What would you have me do?"

While I'm sitting for a minute, the thought comes to mind that I should drag my client into court and sue him to meet my demands.

Although each of us needs to use our own discernment in these matters, this "guidance" doesn't strike me as being inspired by God. Instead, it seems to be motivated by anger. It involves an element of punishment. It is conflict-oriented. It doesn't take the other person's feelings into consideration.

Let's say I decide that this initial "guidance" doesn't feel peaceful – it actually increases my sense of distress. Therefore, I continue to sit for a while.

After a few minutes, another thought comes to mind: the thought that I should quit my business activities, and wash my hands of these conflicts.

Although that thought feels a little more peaceful than the first one, it has an element of self-sacrifice. It makes me feel depressed. Because this, too, doesn't feel peaceful, I continue to wait in receptivity for God's guidance.

Eventually a feeling of peace comes over me. An idea then comes to mind – the idea to sit down with my client and discuss our situation. I receive another idea on how to communicate better, and an idea on how to address several business issues in a mutually supportive way. I decide to discuss these ideas with my client, and see how he feels about them.

These final promptings – which came from a sense of peace – seem much more inspired. Are they the final "word of God"? Probably not. They may simply be the beginning trickle of a river of inspiration.

However, these final ideas seem legitimate because of several elements. They are respectful to myself and others.

They aim at resolving conflict. They are practical, and contribute to a sense of peace. Those are elements that I look for in the process of discerning guidance.

To use another example, let's imagine that I have been invited to a family gathering for the weekend. I'm somewhat interested in the gathering, but I'm also feeling that I could use some rest. I turn the decision over to God, and seek His guidance on the matter.

As I sit, exchanging my perspectives and plans for God's, an idea pops into my mind. It goes like this: *I really should go to this gathering. I haven't seen my family in a while. They may get mad at me if I don't go.*

That, in my opinion, probably isn't the purest form of guidance. There are a couple of questionable elements: there is an intellectual feeling of "I should do this," and there is a fear of people getting angry at me. Also, it doesn't produce a sense of peace.

Let's say that I continue to sit, seeking God's guidance. Another thought enters my mind: *Forget about this gathering. I deserve to take time for myself. If people get mad at me, that's their problem.*

That, too, has a few questionable elements. There is a sense of rigidity – even defensiveness – to it. It's built around a sense of separation. It doesn't take anyone else's feelings into consideration. It doesn't give me a sense of peace.

If I continue to exchange my thoughts – including these initial forms of "guidance" – for God's peace, I may find that my thoughts gradually become more gentle and inspired.

Eventually, I may receive thoughts like: *I am sure that it would be wonderful to see my family, but I do feel that I need some quiet time this weekend. Perhaps I can call my family and ask to see them in a few weeks.*

That, in my opinion, is a more inspired idea than the other two. It is more gentle and sensitive to others. It contains a concrete solution that can be discussed with the people involved. It is self-respectful, but not at the expense of someone else. It does give me a sense of peace. Therefore, it is probably closer to the mark.

As I said above, I think that each of us needs to learn what works for us in matters of discernment. I feel that it's especially important to stay open to new promptings – even if we think we've received something inspired.

God does not speak once, and then leave it to us to figure out how to put His suggestions in place. God speaks to us eternally. If He prompts us to do something, He will tell us how to accomplish it. He will correct the mistakes we make, and guide us around new difficulties.

However, it is essential that we stay open – otherwise, we'll miss out on His new inspiration as we move along.

An Inner Search

So far, I've focused on identifying our "blocks" to receiving guidance, and offering those blocks to God to be removed. Although I find this approach to be effective, it may be helpful to add a more feeling-oriented component.

I'd like to present another exercise – a guided meditation of sorts – that incorporates our intuitive, feeling skills. I encourage you to read through this exercise and then adapt it for yourself in whatever way feels comfortable. There's nothing special about the actual words or images I use. If you are comfortable with the general approach, feel free to apply it as you see fit.

Step 1. To begin, choose an area of your life that is causing you some conflict. It could be a "big" issue or a "little" issue – either one is fine.

Step 2. Let's become willing to give this issue over to God – along with any thoughts about it. Let's say:

God, I want to open my mind to you.
I place this issue in your hands.
I give you all my thoughts about it.
My mind is open; I do not know what to think.

Step 3. Now let's close our eyes and begin to search our minds for a spark of warmth. We're looking for a feeling of comfort, or peace. If any anxious thoughts enter our minds, let's give them over to God and return to our search. We're seeking a sense of comforting warmth.

The Course promises that this warmth is somewhere in our minds. It is obscured only by our personal thoughts. As we quietly sit, let's continue to clear away our thoughts as if they were dusty cobwebs. We want God to take them, and lead us toward an inner sense of warmth.

We may get in touch with this sense of warmth very quickly. Or we may have to search around for quite some time, continuing to give over our personal thoughts to God. Either approach is fine; we're simply asked to make the search.

Once we do begin to feel a sense of warmth or comfort, let's move toward that place in our minds. As we approach the sense of warmth, let's let it grow in our awareness. It might feel like a lovely campfire that we've found after a cold journey through the woods. Or a beautiful sunrise that ends a long night.

Let's sit with this sense of comforting warmth and allow it to surround us. It is peaceful; it is kind. It fills us with a sense of gentleness. As we sit with it, let's realize that we don't want to return to our cold and dark wanderings. We don't want to enfold ourselves in our own darkened thoughts. We want to stay with this warm, gentle light.

After a minute or two, let's open our eyes – and continue to feel the presence of this light. It does not go away when we return to our activities; it only seems to diminish when we place other thoughts before it. Let's try to spend the next few minutes engaging in our normal activities, but keeping this sense of warmth in the forefront of our awareness.

We may also wish to turn our attention to the original issue we held in mind, and allow the sense of warmth to enfold that issue. We're not seeing it through the darkness of our own thoughts anymore. We are seeing it through peace.

If any new perspectives on the original issue come to mind, let's make a note of them. If not, let's simply continue to maintain this sense of warmth in our awareness. The real goal of this exercise is to enter into a sense of God's comforting peace. That is what we're really seeking, regardless of what seem to be the outer details of our issue.

This type of exercise takes a very different approach to "receiving guidance." Instead of trying to "get" insights, we're seeking a state of peace, and then extending that peace outward. This will very likely alter our perspectives on the original issue, and allow our minds to open more fully to God as we go forward.

This type of exercise draws on our capacity to be emotionally sensitive. In it, we are like explorers – we allow ourselves to be gently, even intuitively, drawn toward a place of wisdom and light.

We follow this pull through our own little thoughts and feelings to the inspired thoughts and feelings of God. It can be a relaxing process, if we allow ourselves to be led.

I believe that our minds want to return to this place of comfort. If we unleash them from their habitual thought patterns, they will find their way home. We simply need to loosen our grasp on our normal ways of thinking.

Focusing the Mind

I'd like to address an issue that I touched on earlier in this chapter – the practice of mental focus. *A Course in Miracles* is very clear about the importance of focusing and quieting our minds. For many of us, this is a difficult process. The Course, however, says that it is important.

Many of us go through our days caught in a whirlwind of thoughts. If we sit down to seek God's peace, we may find ourselves buffeted by one idea after another. Sometimes there are anxious emotions that accompany the swirl of thoughts.

The Course understands this, and offers a variety of exercises designed to focus our minds and lead us into peace. As I've said before, I encourage you to consult the Course itself on this matter. My views on the Course are no substitute for the Course's full approach. However, I am happy to offer some basic ideas.

An early step in the Course's Workbook is the practice of "watching" our thoughts. I find this to be a helpful beginning step. "Watching our thoughts" means that we simply take an inventory of what is running through our minds.

Instead of getting drawn into our thought patterns, we take a few steps back and observe them. This sounds simple in theory, but in practice it can be quite a challenge. The process is like sitting through a dramatic movie, all the while reminding ourselves that we are merely watching a film.

Many of us, when we sit down to spend quiet time in prayer, are swayed by thoughts about our work situation, a relationship issue, a mistake we made earlier in the day, and so forth. We tend to get drawn into these thoughts as if we were watching an engrossing drama. The problem is that this blocks the experience of God's peace – the experience of a miracle.

The Course suggests that we back up a bit, and simply note our thoughts as they move by. We say to ourselves,

"There's a thought about my job. There's another thought about my job. There's a thought about my husband. There's a thought about my car."

As we do this, we place some distance between ourselves and our thoughts. The practice creates a window of opportunity. It allows us to make a change of direction.

The process of watching our thoughts is like moving back a few rows in a theater. When we're up close, the action is all-consuming. But as we slide to the back of the theater, we begin to feel a little less overwhelmed by the swirl of thoughts and emotions.

As we learn to step back from our thoughts and simply observe them, we can then move on to a second step. In the second step, we choose something else to focus on.

The Course encourages us to take a calm, comforting idea and begin to focus our minds on it. The process is like backing up in the theater, and then turning our attention from the movie screen to a lovely flower arrangement in the lobby. This isn't the final step. But it does help us strengthen a change in direction.

Once we back away from our normal thoughts, and begin to focus on a single, peaceful thought, we can then try to move past that single thought into an unstructured experience of peace. That is our real goal – to rest in God's comforting love; to clear a space in our minds for the direct experience of God's peace.

As we feel that sense of love or peace enfold us, we may find that new, inspired ideas come to us. The Course supports this. It doesn't want us to "squash" all thoughts out of our minds. But we do want to step away from our personal habits of thought and make room for God's inspiration.

To borrow a metaphor that others have used, seeking God's peace – or listening for God's guidance – is like learning to feed a bird from our hands. We have to become very gentle and very still.

It may take practice for us to learn how to rest, both quietly and invitingly. Learning to step back from our own jumpy thoughts and orient toward peace can help us move into this state.

I'd like to put these three steps together into a focusing exercise. This exercise doesn't require any writing, and shouldn't take more than a few minutes.

Step 1. Observation

Let's begin by closing our eyes and settling back to watch our thoughts. For at least half a minute (and longer, if possible), let's calmly observe what we're thinking.

Our goal in this step is to make a note of each thought that passes by. Instead of letting ourselves be drawn into a memory of last weekend, let's say, "There's a thought about last weekend," and calmly wait for the next thought.

There is some skill involved in this type of practice. We may find ourselves "lost" in a thought for a while before we're able to step back and merely "note" it. We may find that some thoughts recur over and over. As with all things, the Course doesn't demand perfection in our efforts. It simply encourages us to practice.

If feelings dominate the landscape, we can treat those the same. We can say, "There's a feeling of anxiety. There's a feeling of resentment." In our practice, we aren't denying our thoughts and emotions – but we're not letting them control us, either.

When we feel comfortable with the practice of watching our thoughts, we can begin to focus our minds on something more peaceful.

Step 2. Refocusing

Refocusing our minds is a proactive step. It does take some effort. But it can produce very practical results. Having stepped back a bit from our habitual thoughts, let's now try to refocus our minds on a peaceful substitute thought.

It may take some practice to become comfortable with this. In many of us, there is a tendency to constantly break away from focus. Our minds are like wild little puppies, running after one thing, then another.

The problem with having a mind like a wild puppy is that it obscures a sense of peace. If we're constantly jumping from thought to thought, there is little room for God's inspiration to reach our awareness.

A Course in Miracles offers hundreds of "focusing thoughts" in its Workbook. Each Workbook lesson outlines specific thoughts and prayers to use as a centerpiece in this process. If you are working with the Workbook of *A Course in Miracles*, you may wish to use your lesson title for this step.

If you're not working with the Course directly, you can choose whatever peaceful thought appeals to you. You may want to use an idea as simple as "God is Love." Or you may wish to use a prayer to God: "Thank you for your peace."

Feel free to use one of these two statements, or choose another one that promotes a sense of peace. Then let's begin to repeat this peaceful idea to ourselves. This isn't the final step of our exercise; it's just a focusing technique. It can help us pry our attention loose from the attraction of our personal thoughts.

For a minute or two, let's repeat the idea slowly and calmly to ourselves – perhaps every ten seconds. The movie of our personal thoughts may still be running in the background. However, we're going to refocus on this peaceful statement.

If we find ourselves drawn back into anxious feelings or personal thoughts, let's make a note of them as we did in step one, and refocus on our substitute thought.

Let's do this for at least a minute or two. We can spend a good deal longer on this step if we find that it's helping us to focus.

One thing that we want to watch out for is a sense that we're "drifting" or becoming "foggy." If we feel ourselves losing focus – becoming cloudy or even sleepy – let's firmly bring our attention back to our peaceful thought.

The Course suggests that we will benefit greatly from our efforts to stay alert and focused, even if we find the process challenging.

Step 3. Entrance into peace

After a few minutes spent observing our thoughts and attempting to bring our focus to a peaceful substitute thought, we can try to enter directly into a sense of God's peace.

It may turn out that we can only hold a sense of calm, deep peace for a few seconds at a time. That is fine. Our goal is to keep approaching it as best as we can.

What we're seeking is a sense of comfort. We're seeking an experience of being held safely in the love of God. If we reach this for only a second or two, we have succeeded.

As we attempt to move into this place of peace, we may find that some of our old thought habits are returning. If so, we can repeat the earlier steps. We can note our thoughts, replace them with a calming thought, and once again try to move into a clearer experience of peace.

As I mentioned above, it's important to stay "awake" during this process. We want our minds to be clear and open, not drifty or sleepy.

This exercise does take some effort. The Course encourages us to practice, whether or not we're able to fully reach a state of peace. The more we practice, the easier the process will become.

We shouldn't consider it a failure if we spend the bulk of our time simply watching and refocusing our thoughts. This will strengthen our capacity to focus, even if we don't reach the deep sense of peace we're seeking.

If we are able to reach a state of peace – a place where our minds become gentle and still – we may want to make note of any inspired thoughts that then come through. As I mentioned earlier, the Course doesn't want us to sweep away all thoughts. We're simply trying to make room for God's peaceful, inspired thoughts to enter.

The more we practice exercises like this one, the more focused our minds will become. This will help us in our search for God's guidance. As our minds become clear, calm, and open, we'll find ourselves more able to recognize God's gentle promptings.

Others

A Course in Miracles takes a cooperative approach to the spiritual path. It encourages us to seek the experience of God together. This cooperative spirit can be applied to the process of asking for guidance, as well.

I used to think that I had to go off by myself in order to receive God's guidance – that I had to take a long walk or spend time by myself in prayer. While those are valid approaches, I have found that seeking guidance with other people can provide an enormously helpful "boost."

Let's say, for example, that I'm feeling anxious about a particular situation in my life. I sit down to seek God's guidance, but all I experience are my anxious thoughts.

Later that day, I sit down with a friend and seek guidance together. Suddenly, I don't feel so alone. My anxiety about the situation diminishes. God's guidance immediately feels "easier to hear."

I have experienced this repeatedly. It seems to me that one of the greatest "guidance" techniques at our disposal is the simple act of practicing together. As we seek God's guidance with another person, we increase our sense of spiritual connection and our focus. It is a powerful practice.

Having said that, there may be times when it's not practical to sit down with another person and actively seek guidance together. At these times, we can still use our relationships to help us move forward.

As I discussed in an earlier chapter, we strengthen in ourselves whatever we perceive in others. I'd like to briefly discuss this idea as it relates to asking for guidance.

If we look for a spark of God's wisdom inside someone else, we will strengthen that spark in ourselves. It doesn't matter if the other person is actually aware of that spark. If we hold the faith that God's wisdom is within him or her, we will begin to see it – and feel it – increasingly.

Of course, the opposite is true as well. If we think that those around us are lacking God's wisdom, we'll find ourselves lacking it as well.

The person before us may indeed be feeling distant from God's wisdom. She may be acting in clearly unloving ways. We're not asked to pretend otherwise. But it is our job to hold the faith that she can access God's wisdom within her. As we hold this faith in her, we strengthen our own connection to God's wisdom in ourselves.

If we wish, we can practice this in our day-to-day activities. We can walk into our workplace tomorrow and seek for God's wisdom in those around us. If we do, it's very likely that many people will respond to our faith. We will probably be offered some very inspired thoughts.

Whether or not anything seems to happen on the "outside," however, our own minds are healed by this practice. If we seek God's wisdom in those around us, we will strengthen our own connection to God in the process. Our minds will be healed, for we will see ourselves surrounded by conduits for God, children of God. We will see a potential for greatness in everyone we meet.

As I've mentioned before, the Course doesn't ask us to single-handedly leap into this new perception. It simply asks us to begin to trade our old perceptions for miracles. We can say, "God, I see so-and-so as a rather crazy person. But I'm willing to accept a miracle, an inner healing. Help me to see him as a conduit for your wisdom." As we do that, our own minds are healed.

Opening our minds to the presence of God in those around us is an essential part of the Course's approach. God can speak through the people around us. God can send people to comfort, inspire, and support us. But we need to open our minds to His presence in them.

I'd like to present an exercise in order to bring these ideas to a practical level. This will be the last exercise I present in this book. Like some of the later ones, it doesn't require any writing. However, I have included an example for clarification.

Step 1. Let's choose someone whom we see as irritating, foolish, or actually "dumb."

(ex. This guy at work, John.)

Step 2. Let's review how we currently see this person. Let's spend a minute listing out the various qualities we see in him or her. We can use the general form, "I see _____ (person) as _____ (quality)," although we can add whatever other thoughts we wish.

(ex. I see John as really dumb. He acts like he's five years old. I see him as self-involved, totally immature, and annoying. I have never seen him say or do anything that's the least bit mature.)

Step 3. Let's consider the idea that whatever we see in this person, we're strengthening in ourselves. Because we want to become open to the presence of God within ourselves, we need to become open to God's presence in him.

This person whom we consider to be irritating, boring, or whatever is actually the doorway to our experience of

God's wisdom. As we open our minds to a different view of him, we will open our minds to God's presence in ourselves.

Realizing this, let's say:

God, I don't currently see your wisdom in this person.
But I am willing to be shown it.
I am willing to release my old perceptions of this person.
Help me to see a spark of your wisdom in him/her.

Then let's spend a full minute exchanging our view of this person for a new, inspired view.

If we find this step challenging, we can aim for the point at which we simply say, "God, I have no idea how to see this person." That is the crest of the hill. Once we hit that point of open-mindedness, God will guide us forward.

Let's remember that we don't have to "force" ourselves to adopt a new vision. We are simply asked to offer our old thoughts to God and stay open to something new.

Step 4. If we are able to sense a hint of wisdom in this person – a wisdom that the person may or may not have actually exhibited – we're doing well.

Again, we're not trying to pretend that this person's current behavior is saintly, or even proper. We're simply opening our minds to the possibility that there is a potential for wisdom in him that we (and perhaps he) haven't yet seen. This will open our minds to our own potential.

If we're able to sense a hint of God's wisdom in this person, let's focus on it, and let it grow. As we're doing this, let's continue to monitor any of our old thoughts that surface. If we find ourselves thinking how "foolish" this person is, let's note that thought and give it over to God. Then let's return to the hint of wisdom in him.

If it's helpful, we may want to occasionally say:

God, I want to see your wisdom in this person.
Although I need your help with this, it is my wish.

Let's spend a full minute engaged in this process. We are attempting to give God all our past views of this person, in exchange for a view of God's wisdom in him.

It doesn't matter whether this person has ever acted from this place of wisdom. It doesn't matter if he even knows it's there. We're simply asked to let God strengthen it, in our view.

As I mentioned in an earlier exercise, if we spend most of our time merely noting our old thoughts and giving them over to God, our time is well-spent. This can be a challenging exercise. I find that each step is important – even if we need to spend some time with each one.

Step 5. If we are able to get in touch with a sense of God's wisdom in this person, and we're able to let it grow, we can allow this wisdom to extend to other people, and to ourselves. We may want to think of several other people we know, and see God's gentle wisdom in them. Then let's give over our self-concepts, and let God highlight His wisdom within us.

Let's spend the rest of our time simply resting in this sense of wisdom. God's presence within us is both comforting and intelligent. It knows our needs. It knows what we should say and do. It is available to guide us through our activities in the world, and help us accomplish whatever tasks are before us. We are not alone. Let's rest in this awareness, feeling the comforting presence of God.

Summary

The Course promises that God's guidance will help us with all the areas of our lives, from our big decisions to the apparently trivial details. Every time we turn to God for help, we open ourselves to His guidance and also increase our sense of spiritual connection.

In my experience, we are able to recognize God's promptings to the degree that our minds are quiet and receptive. If we're surrounded by a cloud of personal thoughts – analyses of our situation, plans for resolution, and so forth – we will very likely miss God's gentle guidance. God won't shout over our thoughts, but He will reach us as soon as a channel is clear.

Any self-generated thought is a potential block. In this chapter, I've covered several common forms of interference, including our personal perspectives, plans, and goals. However, these are just three flavors among many.

A sense of resentment can be a block to recognizing God's guidance. A belief that we must solve things by ourselves is a block. Any thought that interferes with a sense of quiet, open receptivity is a potential interference.

The Course doesn't demand that we completely rid our minds of these thoughts. It simply asks that we lay them down for a few moments at a time. As we exchange our personal thoughts for a sense of quietness and openness, we may find ourselves inspired to move in a particular direction. Receiving God's guidance can be as simple as that.

A helpful practice in this regard is the practice of focusing our minds. If we have a tendency to jump from one anxious thought to another, we may find it difficult to move into a state of quiet receptivity.

However, as we practice focusing our minds along calming lines of thought, we may find that we can then move into a state of open, unstructured peace. This will help us keep our minds clear as we move forward.

The process of seeking God's guidance isn't, ideally, simply a search for information. It is a practice of placing ourselves in service to God. We open our minds, and allow them to become gentle and still. We trust God to lead us as though we were children. In this way, "seeking guidance" is really an act of faith.

One of the most strengthening habits we can establish is the habit of seeking God's wisdom in other people. God's wisdom is there; we're not merely playing a mental trick. He can inspire us through them just as He can inspire us directly. But our minds need to be open to the possibility that this can occur.

If we believe that the people around us are without God's wisdom, we will find this wisdom harder to access. But if we instead seek for the spark of God in these people, we will draw closer to that light in ourselves.

Conclusion

In this book, I have tried to present a few fundamental themes from *A Course in Miracles*. The Course's central ideas are, in my view, quite practical. They can be applied in numerous ways.

One of the primary practices of the Course is the practice of bringing our dark thoughts to God in exchange for miracles. We bring our pain to God, and He gives us comfort. We bring our confusion, and He gives us clarity. We bring feelings of sorrow, and He helps us feel loved.

It does, of course, take some work to do this. Our habits of thought can exert a strong pull. It takes some effort to reach toward God when we are in darkness.

One of the most helpful practices – and one that I've only touched on in this book – is the practice of turning to God together.

When two people are joined in the goal of bringing their dark thoughts to God, the potential for healing is great. We aren't asked to make a gargantuan effort all by ourselves. We are simply asked to lean on God's strength, and support each other as we go along.

The Course places significant emphasis on relation-ships, whether they are consciously devoted to healing or not. Every interaction that we have with anyone can help us to feel spiritually connected.

I imagine that if we were to travel the world seeking enlightenment, we would find, in the end, that we were surrounded by it from the start. The light we seek is in those around us – our friends and family, co-workers, and the people we pass on the street.

As we open our minds to God's presence in them, we will begin to find that same presence in ourselves. This is an essential practice of *A Course in Miracles*.

Notes

In the previous chapters, I have explored a few of the Course's central themes. In these notes, I'd like to discuss my approach, while providing some references to the Course itself.

As I mentioned earlier, my thoughts shouldn't be taken as a fixed or definitive view of the Course. My perspectives on the Course constantly evolve. Because of this, I encourage you to draw your own conclusions.

I'd like to add that I don't believe that *A Course in Miracles* is for everyone. I love working with the Course; I am deeply grateful for its wisdom and insight. But other people find the Course to be only partly helpful, or not very meaningful at all. I don't think that these people are necessarily "missing" anything.

A Course in Miracles tries to support us in becoming more peaceful, forgiving, and kind. If there is something from the Course that we find helpful in that regard, we can use it. If something else isn't helpful, we don't have to dwell on it.

I find that the Course itself promotes this type of flexibility. For those who are interested, I can recommend reading the Manual for Teachers, Question 24, Paragraph 3, Sentence 4 – as well as Paragraph 6, Sentences 11 through 13 of the same section.

These passages, to me, underscore the Course's remarkable flexibility and practicality. The Course promotes inner peace through practices such as forgiveness and prayer. It's not trying to push philosophical or theological concepts on us. If a specific idea from the Course isn't helpful, we can simply move on to an idea that does help us.

Having said that, I'd like to add that many sections in the Course that used to confuse me now give me a sense of support. In most of these cases, I was, at first, misunderstanding what the Course was trying to say. But as I learned more about the Course's overall thought system, I was able to appreciate the passages in a wider context.

For me, the key to working with the Course has been open-mindedness and a willingness to remain a perpetual learner.

Author's Note

In my author's note, I presented the Course as a program of "spiritual psychotherapy." The Course doesn't refer to itself in this way, but many people have used this description, and I think it's a fine one.

The Course focuses on the process of attaining inner peace through practices such as forgiveness. Although it contains many spiritual ideas, it isn't intended to replace any religion. The Course is simply concerned with the inner process of healing the mind.

Preface

I included the notes on language in the Preface in order to highlight the "background" we bring to words.

Just as we bring images of trees to the word "tree," so do we bring images of God to the word "God," images of peace to the word "peace" and so on.

Because of this, communication can be a tricky business. I generally find it easier to discuss the ideas of *A Course in Miracles* with someone on a one-to-one basis, rather than through a book. Speaking one-on-one, I can get a sense of a person's language and try to present the Course's ideas in a meaningful way.

When writing, however, I have no idea of the background of the reader. That is why I felt that it was important to explain a few of my language choices up front.

Chapter One: Introduction

Trying to describe the Course's use of the word "miracle" in a few sentences was one of the greatest challenges in writing this book. However, even the Course itself gives a very broad definition of the word.

The first few pages of the Text describe fifty "principles" of miracles, and taken together, they cover quite a lot of ground. It may be that describing the experience of a miracle is like describing a feeling of love – you just can't do it in a word or two.

I settled on descriptions of miracles as "inner healings," "experiences of God's love," and "transformations of our thoughts and perspectives" based on the first few pages of Chapter 1, as well as later passages. It might be more precise to say that miracles are the actual thoughts of God (or the Holy Spirit) that foster the inner healing.

Many students of *A Course in Miracles* define a miracle as simply a "shift in perception." I support that definition for those who find it helpful. However, I feel that it's important to keep in mind that this shift in perception is directed by God (or the Holy Spirit), not by us.

I also think that it's important to realize that a miracle isn't any old shift in perception; it is a profound healing. It is an experience of reconnection with God. It is an inner flood of God's peace and love. It can alter our entire experience of the world in a moment.

Our Part in the Process

In this section, I touched on the important idea that we choose (or at least condone) our thoughts. God won't "override" our personal thoughts with miracles. If He did, we wouldn't have free will.

One nice passage on this subject is in the *Psychotherapy* pamphlet (an official "supplement" to the Course), Part 2, Section 1, Paragraph 3, Sentences 3 and 4. This passage, along with others in the Course, points to God's profound respect for our choices.

Giving and Receiving

The main idea in this section – that what we give to others, we strengthen in ourselves – is found throughout the Course. It is, in my opinion, one of the Course's most central themes.

Two of my favorite Course passages on this idea are Workbook Lessons 108 and 187.

I included the story about the attorney and her father in order to illustrate the process of first turning to God to receive a miracle, and then extending it. This approach is inspired in part by Workbook Lesson 154, which highlights the importance of receiving (from God) in order to truly give (to others).

Application

In this section, I focused on the importance of applying (rather than just reading) the Course's ideas. The "What It Is" section of the Preface to *A Course in Miracles*, Paragraph 2, highlights this. The first paragraph of the Introduction to the Workbook also covers the idea that both theory and practice are important.

On a related note, I'd like to add that I sometimes speak with people who understand the Course's ideas but struggle to "make them real." I have found myself in this position at times.

My typical suggestion is to try the Course's disciplined practice of prayer and forgiveness – a practice outlined in the Workbook lessons. That forgiveness and prayer practice is, in my opinion, the real work of the Course.

An Exercise

The exercise that I presented in this section is the basis for many of the later exercises. It's meant to be a template of sorts.

I based the exercise on the general flow of some of the Course's early Workbook lessons. In these lessons, we begin by acknowledging our current thoughts, and then we open our minds to receive God's higher thoughts.

This process can be easy or difficult, depending on our current level of readiness. We may have an area of our lives in which it's easy to exchange our thoughts for miracles. One minute of open-minded prayer may be enough "work" to last a lifetime.

There may be other areas where we are so locked into our old ways of thinking that it takes a great deal of practice to open our minds to an inner healing.

This is one of the reasons that I enjoy working with the Course. The Course doesn't say, "Get it right the first time." Instead, it says, "Keep on practicing."

The Course acknowledges that we may need to keep plugging away for a while; it encourages us like a good cheerleader would. And yet it also maintains faith that an inner shift – an acceptance of a miracle – can happen at any instant.

Near the end of this section, I wrote that the Course encourages us to be honest about our emotions – that they can be used as a barometer to indicate what we're thinking. This idea is touched on in the Text, Chapter 23, Section 2, Paragraph 22, Sentences 6 through 13.

Thoughts and Emotions

The central idea in this section – that our thoughts about (or interpretations of) an event, rather than the event itself, lead to our emotions – is mentioned in the Manual for Teachers, Question 17, Paragraph 4, Sentences 1 and 2.

I'd like to add that this idea is covered extensively by psychological and spiritual writings other than the Course.

Perspectives

In this section, I talked about how we never really see past our personal "perspectives" on an event. In a way, this is the same as saying that we never see past our *thoughts* about an event.

To say, "God, give me a new perspective" is another way of saying, "God, give me a new way to think about this." The perspectives I'm talking about in this section are the inner type.

A Variation

Near the end of this section, I wrote that we don't have to fight our way through difficult situations as we're working toward accepting a miracle. I'd like to discuss this idea a bit.

When I started working with the Course, I had the mentality of an adventurer, or a soldier. I felt that there was a giant task ahead of me – namely, the task of replacing my inner darkness with something more pure. I felt that I needed to ramp up my strength and plunge through the process.

Unfortunately, that approach didn't work very well. Although I spent huge amounts of time "fighting inner battles," I constantly felt weary. I rarely felt peace, or even a sense of kindness, despite my work.

In retrospect, my problem was that I was putting 99% of the emphasis on me and my efforts, and 1% on God's input. I was treating "spiritual growth" like a personal quest. I thought that I was supposed to drive myself through the process; that my personal efforts were going to make or break things.

That isn't, in my opinion, the approach that the Course recommends. The Course encourages us to be gentle with ourselves as we learn to turn to God for support. The Course wants us to see our part as essential, but it also wants us to trust God with the bulk of the process.

The Text, Chapter 18, Section 4 covers this idea as nicely as any.

Valuation

The ideas in this section are largely inspired by psychological and spiritual writings outside the Course. However, the theme of identifying "blocks" to our experience of the miracle – including personally-valued old perspectives – is certainly in keeping with the Course's general approach.

Ordinary Things

The Course doesn't spend a great deal of time talking about the experience of seeing "ordinary things" through inspired vision. However, it does have a few lovely passages. One of my favorites is Workbook Lesson 28, Paragraph 5, which suggests that we can see something as simple as a table in a way that promotes joy.

The Meister Eckhart quote in this section is from *Meditations with Meister Eckhart* by Matthew Fox. The Walt Whitman quote is from his poem "Miracles," part of the *Leaves of Grass* collection.

Little Steps

The process of taking "little steps" that I illustrated in this section can actually be looked at as a three-step process. Although the Course doesn't outline this exact practice, it does offer similar ones.

We begin by letting God show us the spiritual beauty (or innocence) in someone who doesn't bother us very much. Then we allow God to show us the innocence of someone who troubles us. These first two steps prime our minds to accept our own spiritual worth.

Workbook Lesson 121 outlines a similar practice, though it begins with the "troublesome" person as a first step.

Two Types of Vision

The idea that there are two basic ways of seeing – or two ways of thinking – is a central theme in the Course. Workbook Lessons 78 and 91 touch on the idea that we see the world either through God's miracles, or through our own dark thoughts.

Simplification

In this section, I suggested adding "structure" to our practice of opening to miracles. I'd like to comment on this idea.

The Workbook of *A Course in Miracles* promotes a very structured prayer practice. Many Workbook lessons request that we take a minute to pray – or receive a miracle – at the top of every hour.

When I first started working with the Course's lessons, I found this "request" to be excessive. I generally ignored the hourly practices.

In retrospect, I was misunderstanding the role of these hourly minutes. I felt that they were "work," and I believed that I had enough work to do in my life. But I realize now that these minutes are meant to be the opposite of work. They are moments of rest. They are healing breaks – times of spiritual reconnection.

To take a minute to seek God's comfort is an act of kindness to ourselves. We may have some resistance to this, and the Course acknowledges as much. But I find that as we begin to set aside these minutes of reconnection, we begin to realize how valuable they are.

The Workbook serves like a coach, or a personal trainer. It says, "Today we're going to do so-and-so many practices in this way." It provides some structure, but only until a habit has been established.

Along with the Workbook, the Manual for Teachers Question 16 has some helpful insights on this idea of structure and the development of a practice.

Chapter Two: Introduction

In this introduction, I presented the central Course idea that every moment spent with anyone can lead us forward. This idea is expressed in a lovely way in the Text, Chapter 8, Section 3, Paragraph 4.

The Course doesn't want us to be kind and forgiving toward each other simply because it's a "nice" or "good" thing to do. It wants us to be kind and forgiving to each other because this is how our minds are healed.

Seeing is Strengthening

In the first chapter, I presented the idea that whatever we give to others is strengthened in ourselves. In this section, I present a parallel idea: that whatever we choose to *see* in others is strengthened in ourselves.

This doesn't mean that we should close our eyes to someone's unloving behavior and try to pretend that he or she is acting "good." The Course is simply asking us to see things through a higher vision.

If we ask God for His perspective, we may find unloving behavior re-framed as a call for support. We may begin to comprehend the sense of pain that underlies the behavior, which awakens a sense of compassion in us.

The problem is that many of us run around focusing on the mistakes of others, all the while strengthening those mistakes in ourselves. We can instead ask God to heal our vision of the people in our lives, and thus strengthen a sense of patience, kindness, and innocence in ourselves.

One excellent passage from *A Course in Miracles* on the idea of perceiving-as-strengthening is the Text, Chapter 9, Section 3. This passage asks us to focus on the presence of God in those around us.

The Work

One of the elements in the Course that distinguishes it from other spiritual writings is its focus on identifying and releasing "inner blocks." In that sense, the Course is much like a psychotherapeutic path.

Some people find this aspect of the Course troubling. They say, "We shouldn't focus on our dark thoughts." I certainly agree that we shouldn't fixate on our errors, or on the errors of anyone else. But if we are to let our minds be healed, we need to take a few moments to admit to ourselves where we are blocked.

The process, which I described more fully in later sections, is one in which we identify a block (a grievance, for example), and then immediately offer it to God to be removed. We don't deny our grievances – but we don't "sit" with them either. We take responsibility for them, and immediately ask God to replace them with a miracle.

I don't mean to suggest that this is the only valid approach. There are some people who simply practice kindness in their lives, and never "seek out" inner blocks. I am sure that those people, through the sheer force of their practice, will find complete healing.

There are other people – some traditional therapists, for example – who feel that we should "sit" with our dark thoughts and feelings for a while. I acknowledge that this may work as well; that there may be an intrinsic healing process that kicks in.

However, I myself have found it extremely liberating to practice the active exchange of dark thoughts-for-miracles that the Course describes.

The Text, Chapter 7, Section 8, Paragraph 5, Sentences 5 and 6 outline this process very clearly. This passage asks us to take responsibility for our thoughts, and immediately offer these thoughts to God for healing.

Incidentally, the exercises in this chapter are inspired largely by Workbook Lessons 78, 121, and 134 – three very similar (and powerful) lessons that involve forgiveness.

To Forgive Divine

I misunderstood the Course's use of the word "forgiveness" for years. It wasn't, in fact, until I read the *Song of Prayer* pamphlet (another official "supplement" to *A Course in Miracles*) that I began to understand what the Course meant by forgiveness.

Typically, most of us think of forgiveness as something that we personally do, and something we usually do grudgingly. A friend does something bad, and instead of attacking him, we decide to "forgive" him – at least this time.

The *Song of Prayer* pamphlet presents a completely different view of forgiveness. It teaches that true forgiveness isn't something that we do by ourselves. In true forgiveness, we simply let God's forgiving thoughts enter our minds and flow through us. In other words, we let God's miracles clear away our resentments.

True forgiveness is an inner healing, facilitated by God – an inner healing that clears the way for the outflow of God's love through us. It's not something that we grudgingly "give" to a "bad person." The *Song of Prayer*, Part 2, Section 3 points to this practice.

Closer to Home

In this section, I again addressed the idea of identifying our blocks, or grievances, in order to give them to God. I'd like to reiterate that when we come out of denial about a block, the Course asks us to immediately hand it over to God to be removed.

On a personal note, when I find myself in a state of resentment, I often try to "keep the resentment on the radar screen." In other words, I try not to block out my resentful thoughts with worldly distractions, or "get rid" of them through blame. Clearly, neither distraction nor blame truly heals a grievance.

Instead, I try to stay honest about my resentful thoughts, and offer them to God again and again until I begin to feel a change. Sometimes this process takes quite a long time. However, it can, of course, be done in an instant. The key is our willingness to adopt a new vision.

My brief discussion of denial and blame as two major defenses against healing is inspired by my reading of the Course, as well as *Absence from Felicity* by Kenneth Wapnick (a book about the writing of the Course).

Neutrality

In this section, I addressed the idea that there aren't any truly "neutral" views. We may be blending together benevolent and not-so-benevolent perceptions of a person, but that doesn't really produce a neutral view.

It can, in fact, be helpful to identify the various components of what seem to be "neutral" perceptions. This was my aim in the exercise for this section. Identifying the component grievances that we are harboring toward a "neutral" person can help us recognize the thoughts that need to be changed.

The Course covers the theme of neutrality in several Workbook lessons, including Lessons 16 and 17.

Friends and Family

The Course has much to say on the subject of healing our perceptions of those whom we love – friends and family, for example. I barely touched on the practice in this book because it is such a broad subject.

One of the major practices that the Course promotes is the practice of allowing God to transform our conditional-love-based relationships to a more broad and expansive God-love base. This is done through the healing of our perceptions and the reorientation of our goals for the relationship.

The Text, Chapter 17, Section 5 addresses this process. Also, much of Chapters 15, 16, and 17 touch on this theme.

Acceptance

The Course asks us to focus on a person's core spiritual worth and beauty – regardless of whether the person himself is aware of that core. My discussion of "true acceptance" was intended to illustrate this practice.

The Course calls this the real practice of "charity." The concept is covered, for example, in Chapter 2, Section 5, Paragraphs 9 and 10. Of course, taking a "charitable" view of another person strengthens our ability to see ourselves in a more charitable light.

Going Together

The exercise in this section begins like the earlier ones in the chapter. However, in this exercise I included a final step in which we ask God to give us a new perception of ourselves.

This seems to be a general approach of the Course. We begin by letting God heal our perceptions of others. But then we take the next step, and ask God to heal our self-perception (or self-concept) as well.

Workbook Lesson 121, for example, outlines a process in which we see a light in others, and then see those people offering us the same light. One could say that as we extend God's love to others, we open our minds to God's love for ourselves.

Practical Application

In this section, I tried to describe how broadly applicable the seeing-is-strengthening idea is. We are using it all the time, often without consciously realizing it.

To reiterate an idea that I expressed many times in this chapter, every encounter with anyone strengthens in us whatever we choose to perceive in the other person.

Relationships, therefore, not only mirror our thoughts; they actually give us opportunities to move forward or backward, depending on how we choose to see our relationship partner.

Chapter 3: Introduction

In this chapter, I often referred to the process of listening for guidance as "being open to a prompting." I did this in order to diffuse any sense of pressure to "hear" something from God.

Some people do indeed receive God's guidance as clearly as if they were hearing a voice. However, other people simply feel "inspired" or "nudged" to do something. I don't think the former people are necessarily better off than the latter folks. As long as we have some type of inspiration flowing, we're doing well.

I'd like to comment on another point I made in this section – the idea that listening for guidance is similar to receiving a miracle, or seeing a spark of holiness in a person.

I would go so far as to say that these are three flavors of the same core experience.

Whenever we receive guidance, or let our minds be comforted, or let our perceptions of a person be altered, we're opening to the thoughts of God (or the Holy Spirit). We're allowing our minds to be healed. This is the essential focus of the Course.

The Manual for Teachers, Question 29 describes the process of asking for guidance as a central practice of the Course. I enjoy (and recommend) this section, as it contains some very practical ideas.

Removing Interference

My strategy of removing "blocks" to guidance is not extensively discussed by the Course. However, the general practice of identifying and removing blocks is a fundamental theme in the Course. Therefore, I felt that this approach was in keeping with the Course's orientation.

The idea that we need a moment of inner quiet in order to receive God's inspiration is indeed highlighted throughout the Course. One section that covers this idea is the Text, Chapter 27, Section 4.

Releasing Perspectives

One of the ideas that I presented in this section was the idea that we should aim for a sense of inner peace instead of trying to "get" specific guidance. I wrote, "God's guidance will simply follow that peace."

This idea is inspired largely by Part 1, Section 1 of the *Song of Prayer* pamphlet. The *Song of Prayer* suggests that we aim for an experience of God's love, and trust that the guidance and other things we need will follow from that experience of love.

The process is like putting the horse before the cart. If we receive an experience of God's love, we will find it easier to receive guidance as we go along. But if we aim for specific guidance, and skip the experience of God's love, we may miss out on both. The guidance, says the *Song of Prayer*, simply follows from the love.

Little Things

I'd like to clarify that I don't believe that there are any truly "little" things. It can be helpful to ask for God's help with any area of our lives, no matter how apparently small it may be.

Absence from Felicity, a book about the writing of the Course, offers a few wonderful examples of how seemingly "trivial" matters – where to shop, for example – can be used by God for purposes of healing. Pages 235-236 of *Absence from Felicity* offer an excellent story involving the purchase of a winter coat.

Personal Goals (and Plans)

In discussing the process of exchanging our goals (and plans) for God's, I don't mean to suggest that we should abandon all goals and just "drift" through life.

I made that mistake at first. Once I realized that my personal goals and plans weren't making me happy, I became rather directionless. I abandoned all goals, and simply drifted. At the time, I didn't realize that I could turn to God and seek a new set of goals and plans – a set inspired by Him.

As I mentioned, I believe that God has a plan for each of us. For many of us, God's plans will involve a good deal of both inner and outer work. There may be aims and goals involved in the process.

In a way, the Course is very goal-oriented. It is most definitely not directionless. As an example, the Course speaks at length about making peace of mind our primary goal. It wants us to actively work toward that goal. Workbook Lesson 205, among others, covers this idea.

Distinctions

In the examples in this section, I outlined some "initial guidance" that turned out to be not particularly inspired. I did this in order to highlight the Course's teaching that we may need to keep listening past an initial "pop."

When we sit down to seek guidance, we may receive a first wave of our own personal, or fearful, thoughts. As we let that wave wash over us – and find a sense of peace behind it – we may then find ourselves in touch with God's inspired ideas.

My thoughts on guidance being "peaceful, support-ive, and respectful" rather than "critical, abusive, or controlling" are inspired in part by the Text, Chapter 5, Section 2, Paragraph 7.

An Inner Search

Throughout most of this book, I've focused on "giving over" our dark thoughts to God in exchange for miracles. In this section, however, I presented an approach where we simply "move past" our thoughts and enter into a sense of warmth, or light. I find that the Course supports both of these approaches.

Focusing the Mind

One of the main things that distinguishes the Course from other spiritual books is the Course's rigorous "mind training" program. The 365 lessons in the Course's Work-book provide structure for this practice.

The Course expects that we will find this work diffi-cult at first; it doesn't assume that we will be "naturals" right off the bat. But it does ask us to practice, and trusts that we will find the process easier as we go along.

The three-step process of observing our thoughts, focusing on a peaceful substitute thought, and finally entering into an unstructured experience of peace is inspired by several of the Course's Workbook lessons. See, for example, Workbook Lessons 10 or 50.

I often present this three-step process to newcomers because it is relatively simple, and a person can pace himself or herself in a way that feels appropriate.

The first step is easy – anyone can consciously watch his or her thoughts for a minute or two. The second step requires some attention and effort, but it isn't particularly difficult, either. It can be an interesting exercise to choose a favorite peaceful thought and bring our attention to that thought through repetition.

If we are able to move into the final step – a direct experience of God's peace or love – we're doing great, even if this experience only lasts for a second or two at a time.

Others

As I mentioned in this section, I feel that one of the greatest "spiritual boosts" at our disposal is the simple act of joining together. By joining with others in the process of receiving guidance, we strengthen our own sense of God's presence within.

Of course, we don't need someone to physically sit down with us in this practice. If we simply reach out to the truth in another person's mind, we will strengthen our ability to find that truth in ourselves.

Conclusion

I have only covered a small number of the Course's ideas in this book. If there are ideas that you would like to see addressed in more detail, feel free to contact me via www.DanJoseph.info. Thank you.

About the Author

Dan Joseph works extensively with *A Course in Miracles*, leading study groups and spiritual retreats. For the past ten years, he has provided consulting services in various technology and communication fields.

If time permits, Dan would be happy to answer questions about *A Course in Miracles*. You can contact him via his website at www.DanJoseph.info.

If you would like additional copies of *Inspired by Miracles*, you may ask your local bookseller to carry the book or call (800) 758-5761 to place a direct order. Thank you for your interest.